Life and Death
in the Mesolithic of Sweden

Mats Larsson

OXBOW | books
Oxford & Philadelphia

Published in the United Kingdom in 2017 by
OXBOW BOOKS
The Old Music Hall, 106–108 Cowley Road, Oxford OX4 1JE

and in the United States by
OXBOW BOOKS
1950 Lawrence Road, Havertown, PA 19083

Paperback Edition: ISBN 978-1-78570-385-0
Digital Edition: ISBN 978-1-78570-386-7 (epub)

A CIP record for this book is available from the British Library

Library of Congress Control Number: 2016960387

Printed in the United Kingdom by Hobbs the Printers

For a complete list of Oxbow titles, please contact:

UNITED KINGDOM
Oxbow Books
Telephone (01865) 241249, Fax (01865) 794449
Email: oxbow@oxbowbooks.com
www.oxbowbooks.com

UNITED STATES OF AMERICA
Oxbow Books
Telephone (800) 791-9354, Fax (610) 853-9146
Email: queries@casemateacademic.com
www.casemateacademic.com/oxbow

Oxbow Books is part of the Casemate group

Front cover: Burial 41, Skateholm (Source: Larsson 1984)
Back cover: Double burial, Tågerup (Source: Karsten & Knarrström 2002)

Contents

Preface vii

Introduction ix

1   **The Mesolithic Period in Sweden: An Introduction** 1
    Mesolithic on the move 4

2   **Hunters in the Forest** 7
    Ageröds mosse 11
    Settlement patterns and hunting/collecting strategies 14
    Life and death 15
    The end of the Mesolithic in Scania 19
        Segebro: an early Atlantic settlement at the coast 19
        Ageröd V: an Atlantic bog site 20
        Tågerup: settlement and burials 23
        The old woman 23
        The double burial 23
        The man's grave 24
        Yngsjö and Årup 28
    The Last Hunters: the Ertebølle Culture 28
        Soldattorpet, Limhamn 30
        Löddesborg 31
        Skateholm 31
    Tågerup 36
        Houses and burials 36
        Bredasten 37
        Yngsjö 40

3   **Blekinge: New Discoveries** 41
    Bro 597 43
    Damm 6 44
    Norrje Sunnansund: tons of fish 44
    Lussabacken norr 48

4 Hunters along the Kalmar Strait and on Öland 49
   Tingby, a much discussed house 49
      New excavations at Tingby 52
      Concluding remarks 52
   Öland 53

5 Seal Hunters on Gotland 55
   Taking care of the dead 55

6 Into the Forest: Early Hunters in the Southern Swedish Interior 59

7 Pioneers: Hunters in Eastern Middle Sweden 61
   Östergötland: new discoveries 61
   The Mjölby sites 63
      Mörby 63
      Sand covered houses: Högby 64
      Storlyckan: another site with a dwelling structure 66
      The hut 67
      Spatial distribution 69
   Western Östergötland, Lake Tåkern 71
   Sites around Linköping 71
   Life and death around Motala 74
      Strandvägen 74
      House 1 75
      House 2 75
   Death in the lake 77
   The Late Mesolithic in Östergötland 79
   Pioneering hunters: some remarks 79

8 Pioneers in the Early Archipelagos of Eastern Middle Sweden 81
   Early sites 82
      Peak 85 82
      Sites on the A73 84
   Late sites 85

9 Moving Inland 87

10 The Western Part of Sweden 89
   The earliest sites 90
   Hensbacka Culture 90
      Inland sites 92
   Sandarna Culture 93
   The dead 100

The Late Mesolithic 101
   Lihult 101
      Lihult inland sites 102
   Transverse arrowheads 103

11 Moving North **105**
   Leksand 106
   Along the coast: further north 109

12 Pioneers in the Interior of Northern Sweden **113**
   The earliest sites 113
   Later Mesolithic 115

Epilogue **121**

References **123**

Preface

"What a long strange trip its been" (Grateful Dead)

Yes, it has really been a long, and sometimes strange trip. When I started to write this book a year ago I really had no idea of how difficult this undertaking would be. I thought that I had a rather good idea of the publications and site reports. What a mistake! Over the last 20 or so years a vast amount of new and important sites have been excavated and published in different ways, either as articles, books or site reports. Well I managed, I think, to get it right in the end. Sweden is a large country with a lot of archaeology going on in every corner of the country. If something is missing I am to blame and no one else.

I would like to thank a lot of people but they are too numerous to get a mention here but I would especially like to thank the following though for discussions over the years: Lars Larsson, Kristina Jennbert, Bengt Nordqvist, Christina Lindgren, Tom Carlsson, Fredrik Hallgren, Fredrik Molin, Michel Guinard and Per Karsten.

This book is dedicated to my, as always, supporting wife Ylva, my children Per and Malin and my son in law Stefan and my daughter in law Ellinor. But most important my wonderful grandchildren: Maja, Måns and Lobelia!

Thanks!
Linköping 16 April 2016

Introduction

A couple of years ago I published a book about the Swedish Neolithic and as this went down quite well I have decided to write another and this time about the Mesolithic. Of course you could say that this is the wrong order but I am sure that it really does not matter that much. I have had plenty of time thinking about how to do this one after I did the last one. Why not write a new book but about the Mesolithic? As with the Neolithic book the target audience would be archaeology students and archaeologists in general, as well as other interested readers. I also began pondering over what I would include in this book as Sweden is a large country with very diverse conditions and research traditions (Fig. 1).

The extensive number of studies during recent years and the abundance of significant new results also meant that the choices were not very easy or self-evident. It is impossible to describe in detail or discuss the quite extensive archaeological material we have today from the Mesolithic, therefore, I have chosen to discuss fundamental research perspectives

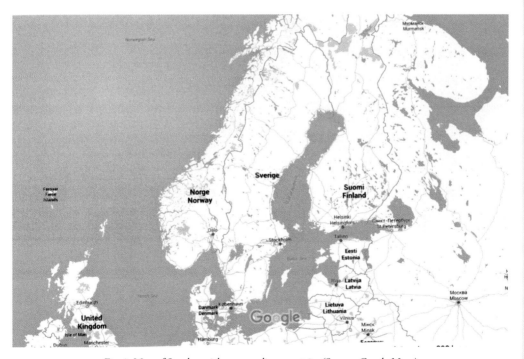

Fig. 1. Map of Sweden with surrounding countries (Source: Google Maps).

concerning the period. I have chosen the sites with this in mind. Thus, it is not a coincidence that I focus on Southern and Middle Sweden, though the country's northern regions are in no way forgotten.

In order to make it easier for the reader, the book is chronologically structured and the individual chapters are thematically organized. The journey begins in the Early Mesolithic and ends with the transition to the Neolithic many thousands of years later. I hope that the book will provide an introduction to the interesting and long period of the early Stone Age, and that it will encourage the reader to pursue further studies in the subject.

At the end of the book, you will find a bibliography of the literature on which my story is based.

Period	Timespan BC
Early Mesolithic	9700–7000
Middle Mesolithic	7000–6000
Late Mesolithic	6000–4000

Unless otherwise stated all date ranges cited in the book are based on calibrated radiocarbon dates.

1 The Mesolithic Period in Sweden: An Introduction

The Ice Age was finally gone. The melting of glaciers and polar ice resulted in dramatic changes in the relationship between land and sea. Öresund and the Danish straits were formed, which led to an inflow of saltwater into what are today known as the Baltic Sea The salinity was approximately two to three times greater than in the Baltic Sea of today, which resulted in a much more species-rich marine fauna (Fig. 2).

In Southern Scandinavia the end of the Ice Age is characterized by the dramatic breakthrough of the Baltic Ice lake at Billingen in Middle Sweden. This happens around 9600 BC. The Baltic has then undergone different stages. The next stage, the Yoldia Sea, began. During this stage, the Baltic was connected with the ocean through an east–west strait across the middle Swedish lowland. A salty southern stream found its way into the Baltic basin, creating brackish conditions that persisted for a few hundred years before land upheaval closed this connection at *c.* 8800 BC. During the Yoldia stage, many of the species of plants and animals that we find in the present day Baltic arrived, like Ringed seal and Grey seal. These species soon became trapped when the connection came to an end and the next stage, the up-dammed Ancylus Lake, began. This freshwater stage, initially characterized by transgressions in the southern part of the Baltic basin, lasted until 7000 BC. Slight intrusions of saline water took place from 8000 BC, influencing only the southern Baltic. It was not until 7000 BC that the ocean's level rose above the southern thresholds and saline water entered the Baltic on a large scale. The salt Litorina Sea was created, which gradually has emerged as the present day Baltic

This period, when the Litorina Sea was formed, is called the Atlantic period (Fig. 2). Between 7000 and 6000 BC we can see a marked rise in sea level. It lasted *c.* 600 years. Large areas were flooded and this must have made a huge impression on people at the time.

During the long period of time covered by the Mesolithic, radical changes took place regarding both natural conditions and settlements. The early period, from *c.* 9700 BC is called Preboreal and was followed by the Boreal period, which lasted until *c.* 7000 BC. The Atlantic period, that followed, lasted until *c.* 4000 BC. The climate changed to warmer and moister conditions. We can blame this on changes in the relationship between land and sea. The forest that had covered Southern Scandinavia for a couple of thousand years slowly changed into what has been called the lime tree period. The forests were now dominated by a selection of valuable broad-leaved species like lime. The Atlantic was also the warmest period after the Ice Age and at the end of the period the warm climate culminated. After 4000 BC

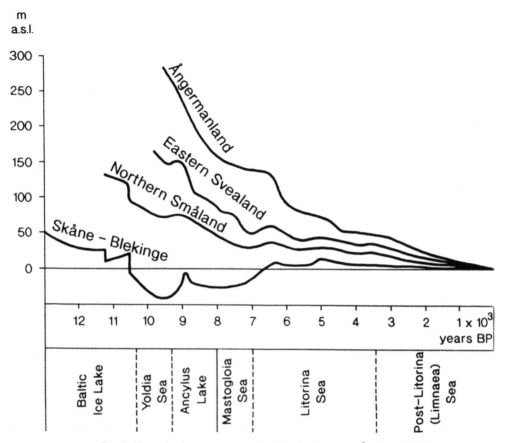

Fig. 2. Shore displacement curves for Sweden (Source: Åkerlund 1996).

we can see a slight deterioration in climate. During this long time-span Scandinavia changed from a tundra landscape to one covered in forest.

People became highly skilled in making a series of diverse stone implements during the Mesolithic. Their skill was developed over centuries and well adapted to life in the dense forests. For archaeologists the microliths they produced are very important as their morphology changed over time so they can be used for dating purposes.

***

I will begin with a brief overview of the history of research into the Mesolithic in Sweden.

As early as the middle part of the 19th century, through investigations into kitchen-middens, archaeologists had been able to distinguish an older phase of the Stone Age. The basis for much of this research was the so-called *Kökkenmöddinge Kommissionen* (Kitchen Midden Commission) that conducted excavations at, for example, Ertebølle in Jutland (Denmark). These excavations were highly influential and the combination of stratigraphic analysis and science set the standard for years to come.

An investigation that changed our perception of the Older Stone Age took place in the early years of the 20th century at Mullerup in the Maglemose (bog) on Zealand. Georg Sarauw conducted the excavation. This investigation, that was epoch-making in terms of how it was conducted, gave name to this first Mesolithic period in Southern Scandinavia, the Maglemose Culture. Intensified peat cutting during the First World War on Zealand led to the discovery and excavation of several other peat-bog sites, like Svaerdborg.

In Sweden the *Torvmossekommissionen* (Peatbog Commission) was established in 1905. The intention was to document human activity in the peatbogs of Southern Sweden. Sarauw, who was Danish but moved to Sweden, did much of the initial work. He was convinced that we had the same situation here as in Denmark – sites in the bogs. Investigations in Baremosse in Scania and other places confirmed this notion.

Carl Stadler discovered several sites in Ageröd, close to lake Ringsjön in central Scania, during extensive field walking. He numbered them I–VII. This was prior to the Second World War. After the War Carl-Axel Althin began a 4 year long excavation campaign in Lund (1946–9). Of primary interest was the Ageröd I site. An important factor in the succes of the project was that scientists from other disciplines like quaternary geology and osteology were engaged.

Several causes beyond his control meant that Althin's excavations were never fully published. A volume *The Chronology of the Stone Age Settlement in Scania* was, however, published by Althin in 1954. In this early synthesis, most of the archaeological material known at that point is presented. Lars Larsson, in 1971–3, conducted new excavations at Ageröd I and took the next step in the history of Ageröd.

In *Eastern Middle Sweden* one can easily argue that Sten Florin, who was primarily active during the 1940s and 1950s, dominated the older research. His greatest contributions were studies concerning changes in sea level and at, among other places, *Dammstugan* and *Hagtorp*, which were the first sites studied where, in addition to pottery, axes and flint, worked quartz was also found (Florin 1948). After Florin's time, Stig Welinder had a great influence on research concerning the Mesolithic in the region. During the 1970s, Welinder led a project that resulted in claims that he could distinguish between two partially contemporaneous culture groups, which he called the quartz group and the flint group (Welinder 1977). The former can be said to be typical for sites in what can be called the archipelago region, i.e., today's Södermanland, while the flint group settlements were primarily located in what can be called the mainland region, i.e., the inland areas of Närke, Östergötland and Dalarna. Today we have a much more detailed view of settlement development, and structure, in this region. We have to rely on the shore displacement curve though for the dating of the majority of sites. This means that the oldest sites are situated *c.* 80 m.a.s.l. which indicates a period of *c.* 8600–8200 BC.

In *West Sweden*, studies of the period began with extensive landscape inventories, which facilitated the continuance of the work. Studies of the inventory and attempts at compilation were begun as early as in the 1870s by Oscar Montelius and ended in 1923 with Georg Sarauw and Johan Alin (1923). After extensive excavations at sites such as *Sandarna*, there followed three decades of work systematizing the material. In many ways one can see Åke Fredsjö's dissertation from 1953 as an epoch-making work that resulted in the division of this period in West Sweden into three periods. The oldest was labelled the *Hensbacka Culture*, after that came the *Sandarna Culture*, and finally the *Lihult Culture*. His main issue was that the sites were shore bound and that the higher the location, the older the site must be. In 1965 material from the site *Hensbacka* was published by Nicklasson. This is, together with *Bua Västergård*, one of the most important sites in the region.

The settlements from the later part of the last mentioned period were coastal; however, a new element is that inland settlements were becoming more common. As a rule, inland settlements were found to be located near larger bodies of water. Waterways have always been important in allowing people to move between different locations and settlements as well as for simple ecological reasons. Via waterways, people with boats have been able to access more ecological zones, something that is beneficial in many ways, for example in making and maintaining contacts and for hunting/fishing.

During the last few decades, the view of Norrland's older Stone Age has changed markedly. From seeing the region as a more or less late-colonized region, today we know better. During the last decade several very early sites have been excavated in the northernmost past of Sweden. We have sites that are radiocarbon dated to between 7600 and 8600 BC. They are situated really close to the receding ice cap. In order to gain a better perspective regarding development here, it is worth mentioning the sites with finds of so-called blade cores, which in South Scandinavia are usually placed in the middle part of the Mesolithic, and have been dated to *c.* 6000–4500 BC. It has often been argued that Norrland's first colonization can be connected to a migration of people from the Norwegian Trøndelag region. This is a very likely description of a complex course of events and therefore the blade core tradition can be associated with development in southern Scandinavia.

In *Norrland,* this tool form has been found at sites like Garaselet in Västerbotten, which has been dated to *c.* 6000 BC. However, Kjel Knutsson has emphasized that the blade core tradition in Norrland should, perhaps, be primarily connected to the later part of the Mesolithic. This is, however, a controversial view.

Mesolithic on the move

During the last decade or so much has happened in Mesolithic research. Most research into the Mesolithic has long been centred on "object research", with dating and cultural concepts as primary components. A "biological" and "economical" orientation characterized much of the earlier research. During this period Mesolithic societies were often portrayed as mobile, nomadic hunting communities with a material culture (i.e. tools and other objects) that were similar across large areas. Great emphasis was placed on ecological conditions and the effect the environment had on settlements. It was not until the 1970s that attention was given to new impulses within research on the Mesolithic. This new research came to be characterized largely by what was later called *New Archaeology*, which clearly focused on economy and settlement structure. An important consideration was how mobile humans actually were. To study settlement function in a food procurement strategy was seen as highly important.

Lewis Binford characterized mobility as either "residential" mobility or "logistic" mobility. The first implies that people moved to explore other ecological niches. The second implies that only smaller groups of people left the base camp for, maybe, the coastal area.

Conclusions were thus often based on studies within social anthropology. In this research tradition it was important to be able to establish social identities and territories. Consequently, studies of material culture were, to a great extent, directed towards such questions.

In the words of Marek Zvelebil: "When prehistorians first defined the Mesolithic and Neolithic at the end of the last century, they could hardly have expected that these concepts would come to mean so many different things to so few people". This quote says a lot about the state of Mesolithic research!

As has been noted that we rarely use the term "Mesolithic period". Instead we tend to use the term "Mesolithic". This term was not actually used until the early 1930s when Grahame Clark published *The Mesolithic Age in Britain* (1932) and *The Mesolithic Settlement of Northern Europe* (1936). The Mesolithic was usually seen as a period of stagnation during which passive societies hardly changed and social relationships were uncontested. Even the champion of Mesolithic research, Grahame Clark, once said that the people of the Mesolithic had "a low level of culture".

During the last decade or so there has been a move away from studying individual sites and their function towards what could be called a more landscape approach. Not only has this approach developed but others have as well. Aspects of burial rites, symbolism, votive offerings, etc, have been promoted. This has resulted in a multiplicity of approaches in Mesolithic research. It is aso interesting to note that the more sites with dwellings we excavate the more complex our interpretations become. From a focus on chronology, procurement strategies and implements we now focus much more on the humans behind the things. Focus is on diversity and variability.

In this time and age, though, the Mesolithic is "On the move" as was the name of the conference volume from the Mesolithic Conference held in Stockholm in 2000. At that conference Stefan Kozlowski stated that "The Mesolithic represents a highly differentiated phenomenon". This is, I hope, something that will be apparent in the chapters that follow.

2   Hunters in the Forest

We will begin our trip through the Swedish Mesolithic in the southernmost landscape, Scania.

Modern studies of Mesolithic settlement in southern Sweden did not develop until after 1940, and then only with obvious influences from British and Danish archaeology, where studies of settlements were connected with scientific investigations in order to create a picture of how people lived and what the landscape they moved about in looked like. This can be directly connected to older Danish studies. With Carl-Axel Althin in Lund a new era in the research of the Mesolithic began in Scania. In 1946 he began systematic excavations of Mesolithic sites, especially in the Ageröd Bog. His investigations at Ageröd were published in 1954. Not only were the artefacts recovered at the site seen as important but also the geological situation, which was of the utmost importance. Both quaternary geologists and zoologists were involved. Althin was very influenced by British archaeologists like Grahame Clark and by the modern excavations conducted by Troels-Smith at Store Aamosen on Zealand in 1944–6.

In the next chapter, a chronological overview of the Mesolithic in Scania is presented. The name of the predominant culture during this period, as well as the Boreal, is the Maglemose. The name emanates from the bog Maglemose on Zealand, where the first excavations of this culture were performed. The Maglemose Culture extends over a long period of time, from c. 9800–6400 BC and has been divided into three phases: early, middle and late. The earliest phase, c. 9800–7800 BC, is characterized by lanceolate microliths; the middle phase, c. 7800–7000 BC, by broad, triangular microliths. During the last phase, 7000–6400 BC scalene triangles dominate.

One question that is often raised is "how many people lived in the region?" It has been suggested that population density during the early Maglemose period was one person per 20–50 km^2, that is to say somewhere between 1600 and 4000 throughout what is now Denmark, Scania and Schleswig-Holstein.

I will start with the earliest evidence dating to the pre-Boreal period. From this period our evidence for settlements is rather limited. We have some but there are actually relatively few sites from the whole of this period in Scandinavia. The oldest site is probably Lundby Mose in southern Zealand. A deposit of bones from various animals such as aurochs, elk and wild boar was found close to the former beach. These had been deposited under water. Some characteristic Early Mesolithic artefacts were found with these bones and the deposit is dated to c. 9800 BC.

From the early pre-Boreal onwards we find a form of settlement that is typical of the Early Mesolithic; a small camp consisting of a hut structure, on layers of gyttja and peat at the edge of an infilling lake. Most of these sites are viewed as seasonal camps or, alternatively, as summer base camps. A couple of these pre-Boreal sites will be discussed further.

Öbacken in south-western Scania is a rather dominant hill in an otherwise flat landscape. On the northern part of the hill, and the northern slope, pre-Boreal and Boreal settlements have been found. A sunken feature was excavated on the highest part of the hill. This has sometimes been seen as a dwelling structure. Among the finds the microliths are the most important element for closer chronological dating. The dominant type is the lanceolate. Of other items core axes and scrapers can be mentioned. The microliths makes it possible to place the Öbacken site in the late pre-Boreal or early Boreal period. A spinal vertebra of aurochs is also worth mentioning. The site can be dated to *c.* 8100 BC.

Linnebjär, north of Lund, was excavated in 1961 and as is an open site. No proper stratigraphy was obtained but as the flint material obviously belongs to the pre-Boreal period it is worth a mention. The site was situated on a small hill, like Öbacken, and with no bogs or streams nearby. The only features found during the excavation were two hearths with soot and brittle burnt stone. The finds assmeblage is not that large but includes core axes, blade scrapers, cores, burins and, altogether, 79 microliths (Fig. 3). Of these 38 are of the lanceolate

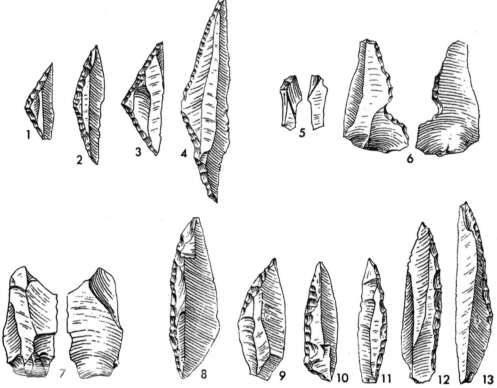

Fig. 3. Artefacts from Linnebjär, Scania (Source: Salomonsson 1965) 1–4, 8–13 lanceolates; 5–7 burins, burin spalls.

type. As there are no radiocarbon dates available we have to rely on the flint material for a date for the site. Based on the lanceolates, Linnebjär should be dated to the late Pre-Boreal/ early Boreal *c.* 7800 BC.

Another area of interest in this context is the *Baremosse* (bog) complex in western Scania. Today this is a bog but in the pre-Boreal/ Boreal it was a lake. Several archaeological and palaeo-ecological excavations and studies have been carried out here over the years. The first to perform an archaeological excavation was Oscar Almgren in 1908. Carl-Axel Atlhin investigated parts of what he named Baremosse I and II in 1949. At the last mentioned site three layers with bark were found. These have, in accordance with Danish findings, been interpreted as floors in three successive huts. The size of these is hard to evaluate but they are certainly small, perhaps a couple of square metres in area. Dating the site is not that easy either. Judging from the lanceolate microliths and the palaeo-ecological dating is should belong to the late pre-Boreal/early Boreal period, *c.* 7000 BC.

We now move to the south-eastern part of Scania, the *Hagestad* area. In this part of the landscape Märta Stömberg conducted several excavations of sites from the Mesolithic to the Late Iron Age as part of the Hagestad Project that began in the 1960s. At two sites, Hagestad 6 and 44, the remains of dwelling structures have been excavated. The sites themselves were situated by the present day Hagestad Bog. During the early Boreal the sea was far away. At the first site four round to oval structures were excavated that varied in size between 3.4–3.8 m long and 2.9–3.4 m wide. Heaths and pits were present in the huts or close by. The date of the huts is based on the flint inventory, which included lanceolates and triangles, indicating an early Boreal date, that is, in the middle part of the Maglemose Culture. There is only one radiocarbon date available; 7904–7518 cal BC (Lu 373 8650±105 B.P), which corresponds well with the flint artefacts.

In the context of the Hagestad huts, another site not far from these is worth mentioning; *Tobisborg* close to Simrishamn. This site is located on sandy soil and differs in this aspect from most hut sites. During the time of settlement, the coast could not have been more than a kilometre away. Here, a couple of features were interpreted as huts. They are not as obvious as the one from Hagestad though. The shape was oval to round and with a diameter of *c.* 3 m they were slightly smaller than the ones mentioned earlier. They should be dated to about the same time as Hagestad.

In northern Scania several early Maglemose sites were excavated during an early part of this century. A site like *Lärkasjöhult 4* is characteristic with a topography that is rather typical for sites during this period. The settlements were situated on small hills close to what was once open water. In the area sites have been interpreted as being both proper settlements, as well as sites for the working of flint and stone and hunting stations. The flint assemblage is not very large but the occurrence of lanceolate microliths as well as conical micro-blade cores clearly dates these sites to an early/middle part of the Maglemose Culture *c.* 7500–7000 BC.

It is also interesting to note that the first quartz site in Scania was excavated on the shores of *Lake Hjälmsjön*. A considerable quantity of quartz was noticed over an area of 10 × 30 m. The assemblage is primarily made up of debris but includes a couple of bipolar cores. The chronology of the site is difficult to evaluate but it ought to be Early Mesolithic.

At *Årup* in north-eastern Scania, settlements as early as the Ahrensburg culture (9500 BC) were excavated in 2002. The late Palaeolithic material was discovered in a sandy layer below the peat. Årup is situated close to the present river of Skräbbeån which marks the eastern boundary of the fertile Kristianstad Plain. The sites at Årup were located close to the shore during the Ancylus stage of the Baltic. The highest transgression level was reached around 8400 BC. This was also an interesting time regarding changes in the environment. The open landscape of the Late-glacial was gradually being replaced by forest.

The sites are situated around 3–8 m.a.s.l. and the Early Mesolithic can be divided into an early phase and a late phase. The early phase is characterized by small flake axes, conical micro-blade cores and lanceolates. In the later phase handle cores, micro-blades and lanceolates are common.

The remains of at least four dwelling structures were recorded as well as two flintworking and one area for the manufacturing of microliths. In the context of this chapter two of the hut structures and one wind break are of special interest. All of the dwelling structures were situated close to the shore of the Ancylus Lake.

At *Site 3* a small, *c.* 30 m^2 activity area was excavated. Clearing by hand revealed the remnants of a roughly 4.5 long and 2.5 m wide hut consisting of four stake-holes, two furrows, a couple of stones and a few clay deposits encompassing an area of about 11 m^2. A hearth was located just outside the entrance to the hut.

The rather scanty quantity of flint is dominated by informal artefact categories like flakes, cores and blades. All are made from the locally derived Kristianstad flint. Of more interest here are the formal tools. Few are present and they consist of two flake axes, two lanceolate microliths, a burin and a flake borer. They all indicate the Early Mesolithic and a radiocarbon date from the hearth places the hut in the period 8300–7800 BC.

The next site of interest in this context is *Site 4*. A round to oval structure, *c.* 8.5 × 4 m and orientated south-west to north-east, was found adjacent to a microlith manufacturing area. The feature, which has been interpreted as a hut, was made up of 17 stake-holes, three pits and two furrows. The living space was *c.* 30 m^2. It was, like the hut discussed above, to close to the former lake shore. Taken together with the production area, site 4 is interpreted as a small, temporary, settlement site. Site 4 can be dated to an early part of the Maglemose Culture based on the lanceolate microliths found in the production area.

It is noticeable that, on this site, Early Mesolithic huts have been excavated; these are a rare commodity in Southern Scandinavia. There is also a high degree of variability in the shape and size of the huts: oval to round and 4.5 × 2.5 m and 8.5 × 4 m. This variation might indicate different settlement types, hunting or procurement strategies.

In this context is is interesting to note that at *Ålyst*, on the island of Bornholm, huts similar to the those mentioned above have been excavated. The huts are dated to the Early Maglemose culture; 8280–7970 cal BC (AAR-9831 8870 ± 65 BP) and 8240–7780 cal BC (AAR-9876 8925±65 BP). The dwellings appear to more or less contemporary. We could, in this context, also mention the early sites at *Lake Vesan* in the province of Blekinge, which are discussed in a later chapter.

After this brief visit to the north-east part of Scania we will next move to the central part of the landscape, *Ageröds mosse*. This is a peatbog that is the northern part of a bog complex where the southern part is named Rönneholms mosse. During the Mesolithic the bogs formed a westerly part of the lake Ringsjön.

Ageröds mosse

Before we move on to discuss the actual sites in Ageröd it is necessary to have a brief look at the history of the ancient lake and its development (Fig. 4). During the Late Glacial *c.* 11 000 years ago, Lake Ringsjön was a ice lake that was much larger than it is today. As the climate slowly became warmer a lake was formed in the northern part, Ageröd, and another to the south, Rönneholm. The lakes developed during the pre-Boreal and Boreal, *c.* 11,000–9000 years ago. At the beginning of the Atlantic period the lakes still had open water and, in the clear water, the sedimentation of detritus gyttja began. The next step in the changes in the lake began during the Early Atlantic (*c.* 8000 years ago) when large areas of reed started to expand over the whole of the ancient lake. Together with the overgrowing reed, trees and bushes started to grow up at the edges of the bog. It was during the youngest part of the Late Atlantic, *c.* 7000 years ago, that the high bog started to evolve.

Now it is about time that we proceed to the sites themselves. In 1954 Carl-Axel Althin wrote that Ageröd I was the natural foundation-stone on which to build the chronology of the Mesolithic Age of Scania. This says something about the importance of the site. It lies at the point where the Rönne å (river) flowed from the then lake Ageröd on a moraine mound that was presumably the centre of the settlement. The 1946–9 excavation by Althin took place in the peatbog in front of the site. During the excavation four artefact producing layers were identified at the settlement *Ageröd I HC*. From the moraine up we have a bottom layer (BL), Lower peat (LP), the White layer (WL) and Upper peat (UL). The three first layers all belong to the late Boreal period. I will not go into any great details regarding these layers but worth a mention is the distinctive "*white layer*" made up of weathered sandstone. As mentioned briefly above, it was Lars Larsson from Lund who took on Althin's work and performed his own excavations here between 1971 and 1973.

The occurrence of trapezoid microliths together with a very distinct fabrication of micro-blades, trapezes and handle cores date Ageröd I to the later part of the Maglemose Culture in the late Boreal/early Atlantic. Not only were flint-and stone tools found at the site but also artefacts made of bone such as points including slotted points. There are several radiocarbon dates from the site and they indicate a rather large time span; 7545–7009 to 6804–6779 cal BC.

One of the more intriguing finds from Ageröd is a dwelling structure previously excavated in the 1940s by Althin. It was found in section I: C, above the "white layer", and the structure was built on this layer of sandstone. The sandstone, brought here from a source over 2 km away, stretches for 30 m along the former shoreline (Fig. 5).

The base of the hut consisted of one layer of stones. These covered an area of about 8 × 3 m. Traces of wood were also found probably represent posts. No traces of a hearth were found inside the hut but two were excavated just outside. The "white layer" contained long and narrow triangular microliths as well as a few axes and handle cores (Fig. 6). The dating of the hut should be late Boreal/early Atlantic based on the findings.

If we leave Ageröd for a while and move to Rönneholms mosse there are several interesting sites of a different nature. We can, in this context, mention the small campsite *Rönneholm 29* that was situated in the middle of the ancient lake. Surprisingly it was not situated on a small mound but directly on the gyttja layer. This should indicate a settlement during a low water period. The number of flint tools is small but the existence of handle cores indicates the same period of time as Ageröd I.

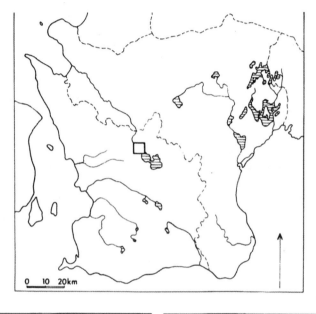

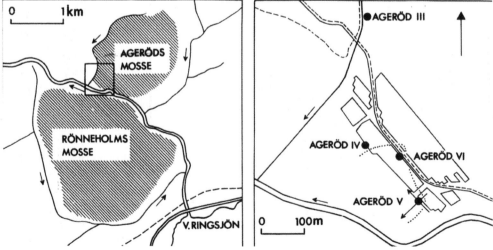

Fig. 4. Maps of the Ageröd area in Scania (Source: L. Larsson 1978a).

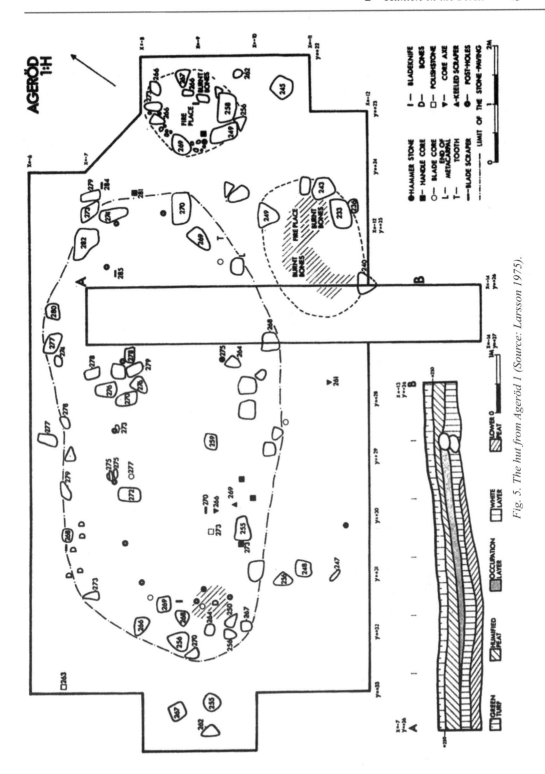

Fig. 5. The hut from Ageröd 1 (Source: Larsson 1975).

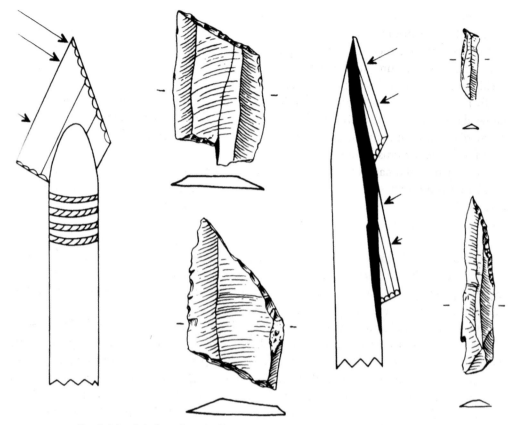

Fig. 6. Microliths from Ageröd I (Source: L. Larsson 1978a) showing methods of hafting.

Settlement patterns and hunting/collecting strategies

It is now time to leave the actual settlements and look at the way people lived and what kind of food they had for dinner.

From Ageröd I the most important species are as follows: aurochs, elk, red deer, roe deer, wild boar. Of these, the most important animal is red deer which, at Ageröd I accounts for between 50% and 75% of the total meat consumption. If we look at the seasonal indicators from Ageröd I it seems that the settlement was in use during summer. This assumption is based on the occurrence of red deer calves and a skull of roe deer with the antlers still in place. Another indicator should be the abundance of hazelnuts at these sites.

One important factor to take into consideration is where did people lived during the winter. Interestingly bones of grey seal as well as amber were found at some of the Ageröd sites. The most likely area for settlement during winter should be the coast of Öresund about 34 km to the west of Ageröd and Ringsjön. It is not easy to understand the development of Öresund though and both Iversen and Mörner have discussed this problem and are of the opinion that the shore-line should have been located 10–15 m below present sea level. Data providing evidence for coastal settlement during the late Boreal/early Atlantic are still very scanty. The evidence that we have from at least a couple of coastal sites, such as Tobisborg and Ulamossen, together with finds of grey seal, indicates that we should expect that the sea was utilized as a resource in the winter. In recent years sites from north-eastern Scania and Blekinge clearly show this settlement pattern.

To help with the hunt the only available animal was the dog. From Danish sites we know about three different sizes of dogs that are roughly equivalent to the Greenland dog, Norwegian elk hound and smaller ones similar to the Laponian Herder. Maybe they were used for different forms of hunting?

The very thin and narrow micro-blades could be used not only for making different types of microliths but they were also used in slotted bone points. The micro-blades were held in place with resin. The length of these bone points could be as much as 25 cm and they were obviously very efficient as hunting weapons.

The development of the bow and arrow was of great importance. Based on finds from many sites in Southern Scandinavia we know quite well what these looked like. They were often made of elm and they had a man's length. The arrows that were used were of different shapes depending on their use. Some were tipped arrows made of small pieces of shaped flint microliths manufactured from flint micro-blades.

One of the more famous finds of Mesolithic arrows emanates from the *Lilla Loshultmosse* bog in north-eastern Scania where, in 1951, a bundle of wooden arrows together with microliths was excavated. On one of the arrows the tip was *in situ*, and was fastened only by a lump of resin over the head of the shaft, without a groove. Actually only one of these arrowheads is a true microlith, the remainder are micro-blades. Two of the arrows are radiocarbon dated to 8279–7794 cal BC (Lu S 7217 98915±80 BP) and 8004–7604 cal BC (Lu-S 8993 7855±60 BP), that is, an early part of the Maglemose Culture.

Just to show how efficient these hunters were with their weapons we can have a look at one of the more famous kills; the *Vig-aurochs*. The skeleton was found in 1904 during peat cutting. It is now on display in the National Museum It has been dated to around 7500 BC. Two of Maglemose hunter's arrowheads are firmly buried in the skeleton. Bone has grown around one arrowhead, so that did not cause the death of the ox and, it must have lived for several years after the hunter's first attack. But the second arrow must have hit it shortly before its death. Some round holes in the shoulder blades have been interpreted as traces of a spear that has pierced the aurochs. It escaped, the hunters followed it and attacked with spears, it fled again, and perhaps ran out on the ice of a small lake – and fell through.

Another famous Danish find is from *Prejlerup*, a few kilometres from the Vig-aurochs findspot where another aurochs skeleton was found in 1983. It was a huge bull with a height of 190 cm, maybe 18–20 years old. It has been dated to 7595–7284 cal BC (K-4130 8410±90 BP).

Life and death

What, then, do we know, not about the dog but about his human master? We may begin in Denmark. As far as we know today one of the oldest examples of known human remains in Denmark, and maybe Scandinavia, was found in 1941 in a small bog at *Koelbjerg* on the island of Funen. The bog was a small lake during the pre-Boreal. The remains are from a woman who presumably drowned. She was about 25 when she died and was only 155 cm tall. A radiocarbon date indicates that she died *c.* 8000 BC.

The woman from Koelbjerg is not alone though. At present we know of three more individuals that are *c.* 1000 years younger, *c.* 7000 BC. At the *Holmegård V* settlement near Næstved (Zealand) parts of an individual have been found in a bog. Skeletal remains from the Maglemose time have also been found in *Køge Bugt* (Zealand).

Looking at the ^{13}C values from these individuals we can see some interesting differences. The values tell us a lot about the diet of these hunters. The higher the ^{13}C value, the greater the proportion of marine resources were present in the diet of the individual. This is exactly the case with the individuals from Holmegård and Köge. They had evidence for both terrestrial and marine food. This is really strange because, in the case of the Holmegård individual, he had to travel *c.* 150 km to be able to reach the coast.

At *Hammerlev* in Jutland a formal burial from the Maglemose period was excavated in 2001. The deceased, who was an adult, had first been cremated. After this the remains of the deceased, together with implements, were laid on a piece of animal pelt and red-ochre was scattered over the top. It was all put in a small pit, *c.* 0.7 m deep (Fig. 7). A radiocarbon date of *c.* 8250 BC makes this the oldest burial in Denmark so far.

Fig. 7. The burial from Hammerlev on Jutland (Source: Museum Sönderjylland).

It is now time to cross the Öresund (strait) and have a look at the Scanian evidence.

One of the more famous burials is that from *Barum* in north-eastern Scania. The burial was discovered during work for a cow path in 1939 and was excavated the same year by Folke Hansen. The deceased was placed in a *c.* 1.2 m. deep pit that was 0.6 m wide. Today it is displayed in the Museum of National Antiquities in Stockholm (Fig. 8). Together with the unusually well preserved skeleton, a slotted bone point, some flints and a bone chisel were found. Based on these findings, the skeleton was seen as that of a man about 40 years of age.

A re-newed examination in 1970 showed that the man was actually a woman 45 years old who had given birth to several children. So the gender was changed. Further examinations in 2000, including both radiocarbon dating and isotope analysis, showed that the woman had died of an infection that caused blood poisoning. The isotope analysis indicates that she had consumed a predominantly terrestrial diet. Radiocarbon dating

Fig. 8. The burial from Bäckaskog in north-east Scania (Source: the Swedish History Museum).

placed the grave in an interval between 7010 and 6540 BC, that is, at the Maglemose-Kongemose transition.

There are other aspects of human life worth discussing further. In the context of the Early Mesolithic the decorated objects made of bone, antler or amber are of great interest as they reveal other aspects of human life and beliefs.

I will begin with some objects from Denmark.

In a bog near *Ryemarksgård* on Zealand an aurochs bone incised with human-like figures was found. It was not made to be a tool, and it was only carefully polished on that part of the bone on which five figures and three parallel zig-zag lines are scratched. They have triangular heads, the legs are just lines and their bodies are shaded. Only one of the people has arms. Three of the figures are seen from the side, and two are apparently seen from the front. The latter have a vertical line through the centre of their bodies, which separates the shadings, like joints in a suit. To the right three parallel zig-zag lines have been scratched with strong lines as though emphasizing something important.

Most authors believe that the figurers show the Maglemose hunters themselves, taken directly from everyday life; some suggest that one figure depicts a pregnant woman, making the bone a kind of fertility amulet.

Another famous image on a piece of antler comes from *Aamosen* on Zealand. The drawing depicts a man and a beast, maybe a deer. Both are drawn in the characteristic geometrical style of the Maglemose period. The drawing is known as "*The Deer slayer*".

Compared to the almost overwhelming number of bone, antler and amber artefacts from Denmark the finds from Scania are few. We know of some similar finds but without depictions of humans. On most of the decorated artefacts from the landscape the decoration could be said to be typical for the Maglemose Culture: drawn thin lines, geometrical patterns and triangles. From *Ageröd* we know of several adzes and axe sockets, only few of them show signs of linear decoration though. Several interesting decorated antler and bone artefacts are known from the site of *Sjöholmen*, located adjacent to the present outlet of Rönne å (river) which issues from the western Ringsjön. The site has been excavated several times over the years, starting in 1929. Among the finds is one antler adze and a couple of decorated antler artefacts. The decoration on these implements is made up of shallow, incised lines, shaded narrow bands, rows of triangles, squares and shaded rhomboids.

It is a strange and lost world that we see on these decorated objects. Like most known hunter/gatherers today we can probably say that the Maglemose hunters' world was based upon a belief that everything in nature was sanctified. Maybe they had religious leaders that could be the equivalent of Shamans. If, for a moment, we look at the known amber pendants and figures, especially from Denmark, and interpret them as amulets worn for protection against evil, we are close to shamanistic beliefs. Some of these amber figures have been intrepreted as depicting bears, swans and wild boar. A study of hunters living today in Siberia by Peter Jordan could shed some light on this. The bear, according to these hunters, is the No. 1 animal in their shamanistic world view. The swan is the bird that carries the soul to the bear. It is interesting to maybe see these amber figurines in the same way; depictions of important animals in a world based on shamanistic beliefs.

The end of the Mesolithic in Scania

In this section I will discuss what was happening at the end of the Mesolithic *c.* 6500–4000 BC. I will focus on some well excavated sites that in many ways tell the whole story including burial customs. The two culture groups that are scrutinized are the Kongemose and Ertebølle Cultures.

We can begin with a look at the *Kongemose Culture.*

During the middle part of the 7th century BC extraodinary changes occurred in the landscape and in the relationship between land and sea. We can, for example, notice that global warming now reached its optimum. This period is called the Atlantic and is charaterized by a warm and moist climate. The forest changed as well into one dominated by lime.

Most noticeable is the rise in sea level which totally changed living conditions for the hunters. Denmark, for example, became a land of fjords and bays. The sea that surrounded Southern Scandinavia had a higher degree of salinity and was warmer than it is today. Because of this, large shellfish banks developed over the centuries.

Changes in the environment meant that the sea shore became the foremost settlement area during the next couple of thousand years. This is the period of the Kongemose Culture, named after a site in Store Åmosen on Zealand. Until now the oldest sites are dated to *c.* 6400 BC. It is during this period that, for the first time, we can document how the hunters used the coast and sea with its abundance of food. The settlements were situated at the coast or in areas more protected by a lagoon. The selected areas are what we could call high-productive biotopes. These sites were probably used during the warmer parts of the year and it is possible that during spring and later in the year people moved to special hunting sites further inland.

The Kongemose Culture has been divided into three phases:

1. *Blak Phase*: *c.* 6400–6000 BC.
2. *Villengebæk Phase*: *c.* 6000–5400 BC.
3. *Vedbæk Phase*: *c.* 5700–5400 BC.

The different phases are named after characteristic Danish sites and this divison is based on rather small variations in the flint industry, especially the arrowheads which, throughout this period, are characterized by what we name oblique arrowheads.

The main settlement area for the Kongemose hunters is Zealand but we have several large settlement sites in Scania that will be discussed further below such as *Segebro*, *Ageröd V* and *Tågerup*. They all have different locations; the first and last were situated by the coast or a lagoon while Ageröd V is located, as were the Ageröd sites discussed in an earlier context, by lake Ringsjön in central Scania.

Segebro: an early Atlantic settlement at the coast

The site *Segebro* is probably most famous for the Post-glacial finds belonging to the Bromme Culture made there in 1960. Equally important though are settlement remains from the early Atlantic excavated over several episodes starting in 1936 and ending in 1976. The site was situated at the mouth of the River Segeå, very close to the coast.

The layout of the site is very difficult to understand, This is due to difficulties in estimating the total area of the site as well as later disturbances. The dominant artefact group are tools made of flint and a closer look reveals that, among cores, only 14% consist of handle cores. This might be strange as the site clearly belongs to the Kongemose Culture. Most common among the tools is the oblique arrowhead. Other tools that occur are borers, scrapers, burins and flint axes. In the last group core axes clearly dominate with 131 examples while flake axes are rather uncommon with only nine. Among tools of antler and bone the most common ones are bone points (23). There are eight finds of slotted bone points as well.

Looking at what the hunters had for dinner it basically comes from three different ecosystems; the dense broadleaved forest, the freshwater habitat of and around the river and the sea coast. The main part of their household refuse consists of remains of red deer, wild boar and roe deer. From the freshwater of the River Sege we have evidence for fishes like perch, zander and others. From the sea we have cod, herring and flounder as well as other species. It is also worth noting that they hunted seal, especially the large grey seal. Based on the occurence of these animals it looks like the settlement was inhabited more or less throughout the year, with a slight increase in the late spring. During the cold months the site seems to have been perhaps not wholly abandoned but only used infrequently.

The chronlogy of the site is not absolutely clear but a combination of typology, especially oblique arrowheads, indicates that it belongs to the Kongemose Culture and radiocarbon dates indicate a period between *c.* 6400–5700 BC.

Ageröd V: an Atlantic bog site

The site *Ageröd V* was first excavated by Althin in 1947 and 1948 and briefly mentioned in a publication by him in 1954. Renewed interest led to further excavations in 1972, and 1977–1980. During the excavations concentrations of stone, tree logs and branches as well as a small depression filled with an abundance of hazelnut shells were found. The last feature has been intrepreted as a pit for the roasting of hazelnuts. The logs and branches might indicate the presence of structures or platforms but today this is difficult to say with any certainty.

Looking at the tools from the site, starting with the cores it is obvious that handle cores clearly dominate the inventory (Fig. 9). Among the arrowheads the oblique forms are most common but there are a few examples of transverse arrowheads as well (Fig. 10). Of other tools we have blade scrapers, borers, burins and flake scrapers. Of the 13 flint axes found at the site all belong to the group core axes.

In relation to the amount of bone and antler found, the number of bone implements is few. A slotted bone point and a couple of bone points have been found. One of the more interesting tools found is a bow. The original length ought to have measured *c.* 170 cm. Other implements made of wood worth a mention are two leister prongs (fishing spears). There are also parts of wicker cages, probably fishtraps.

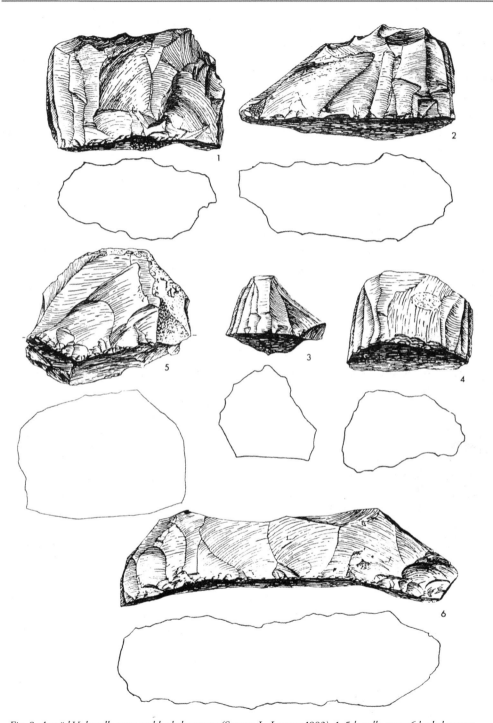

Fig. 9. Ageröd V: handle cores and keeled scrapers (Source: L. Larsson 1983): 1–5 handle cores; 6 keeled scraper.

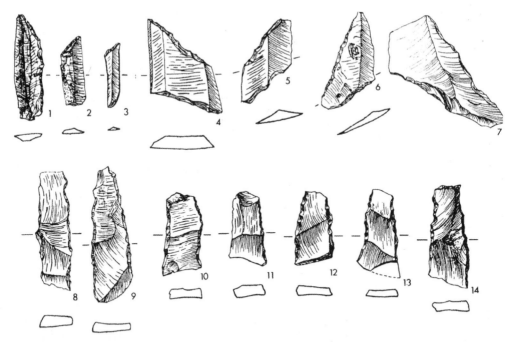

Fig. 10. Ageröd V: 1–7: oblique and 8–14: transverse arrowheads (Source: L. Larsson 1983).

The very thorough dissemination of the distribution of tools have led to two models for the occupation of the site:

1. The site has been occupied on several occasions.
2. The site has been occupied on only one occasion. During this visit activities have been assigned to different parts of the site.

The excavator, Lars Larsson, sees the second model as the most plausible here.

Now it is time to look more closely at what the inhabitants fed on. According to the bone material the hunting of red deer, elk and wild boar and fur-bearing animals such as marten, otter and maybe brown bear has been conducted. Of these red deer clearly dominates. If we look closely at the fish assemblage it seems that bream, pike and perch are the most important species. Seasonal indicators are important in a discussion of hunting and settlement. Regarding Ageröd V there is no single answer to the question of seaonality. The indicators show limited settlement during spring, with an intensification during the autumn. Pollen, macroscopic plant remains including wood and charcoal, bones from mammals, birds and fish, as well as insect remnants were all analysed. The plant and insect remains provide a relatively detailed picture of the local environment around the settlement at the time. This points towards an environment with great biological diversity that would have been optimal for a hunter-gatherer culture. This rich environment is reflected in a very concrete manner in the identified bone material listed above. Hunting was supplemented with snared birds and fish from wetland areas which, during this period, largely comprised a lake.

Regarding Ageröd V, the occurrence of handle cores and oblique arrowheads clearly indicates the Kongemose Culture. Based on the studies of oblique arrowhead mentioned earlier it seems that it is the Vedbæk and, to a lesser extent, Trylleskov phases that are important here.

Several radiocarbon dates exist from the site and they have a distribution of *c.* 5890–5500 BC. These indicate that the site is a little bit younger than Segebro.

Tågerup: settlement and burials

The site *Tågerup*, in western Scania, was excavated in 1998. It was situated on a promontory in a bay into which flows the River Saxån and is a very protected place. Along the bay we have evidence for several Mesolithic settlements of which a couple were excavated ealier in the 1960s and '70s.

In what was once the seashore an abundance of wooden posts had been hammerd down into the ground. They had probably been used as tethering posts for canoes but also for fishing traps.

The excavation, totalling 23,000 m², was divided into two trenches, east and west. The western trench contained the Kongemose remains and is discussed here.

The finds assemblage from the excavation is huge: 234,168 units of flint were documented. Of course it is not possible, in this context, to discuss every piece of flint or even artefacts. For a further discussion the books from the excavations are recommended (Karsten & Knarrström 2002; 2003).

Characteristic of the site, and the Kongemose Culture more widely, are the long, symmetrical blades. These make up about 15% of the total number of flint artefacts. Punches were used in the production of these long blades and the majority were struck from handle cores or on sided blade- cores. Several types of flint arrowheads were discerned: trapezoid microliths, rhombic microliths and oblique transverse arrowheads (Fig. 11). The oldest ones are the trapezoid ones that ought to belong to the Blak phase. Of bone and antler, we find slotted bone points as well as other forms of points.

Of great interest also is the small burial ground that was found on a small plateau overlooking the settlement. A total number of seven burials was excavated, in which skeletons were preserved. The total number of graves must once have been much larger. Some of the burials will be discussed.

The old woman

In grave 1 a woman of about 50 was found. She had been placed in a supine position with her head to the west. There were no gravegoods (Fig. 12).

The double burial

In grave 5 were discovered a couple, both aged about 45. They were about 1.66 m in height and both lay outstretched on their backs. One is probably a man and the other a woman but

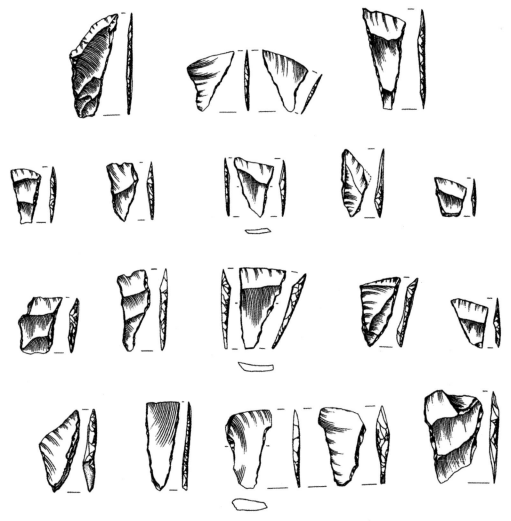

Fig. 11. Tågerup: Transverse and oblique arrowheads (Source: Karsten & Knarrström 2002).

there are some uncertainties involved in the classification. If the northern individual in the grave is a man he had an impressive array of tooth beads of wild boar, seal and elk adorning his chest. A slotted bone point was found in his abdominal area. This is one of the more spectacular finds from the site (Fig. 13).

The man's grave

This man was between 40 and 50 when he died. The skeleton is unfortunately poorly preserved. He had been stretched out on his back.

Another side of ritual behaviour is the votive deposits. Close to the burials were found two bone pins and a large conical flint object. They had been deposited next to a 0.3 m

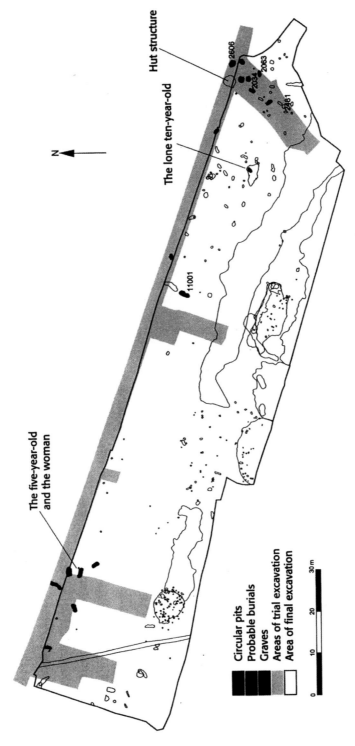

Fig. 12. Tågerup: plan of graves, Kongemose burials indicated (Source: Karsten & Knarrström 2002).

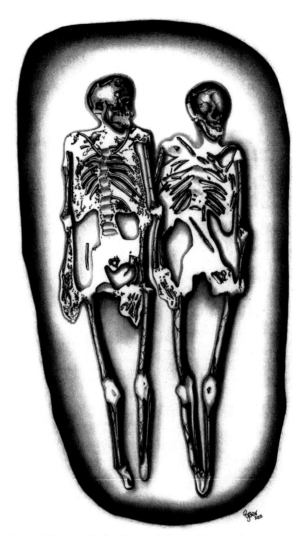

Fig. 13. Tågerup: the double burial (Source: Karsten & Knarrström 2002).

diameter large stone and should be seen as a closed find of a votive character. Another object that should be put into the same category is a well preserved axeshaft, 39.5 cm long, made of red deer antler. This was found at a depth of 3.5 m in the eastermost part of the Kongemose settlement. The shaft is basically decorated with two parallel lines. These rhomboid figures are carved in sequences of varying length so that they form continuous bands. There are also zig-zag figures and short parallel strokes visible on the shaft (Fig. 14). The message on the shaft is hidden from us today but, as the excavators write, maybe it should be understood as a message from them to us? The shaft has been dated by radiocarbon to an early stage of the Kongemose Culture, *c.* 6300 BC.

It is now time to have a look at the diet of the people that lived on the promontory at Tågerup. Judging from the number of bones, fish seems to be the dominat food, but in comparison with a red deer you need 150 cod to get the same amount of food. Seven analyses of ^{13}C values were performed on both human and dog bones from the site. These show that people mainly consumed food from terrestrial sources. The terrestrial mammals are, to 86%,

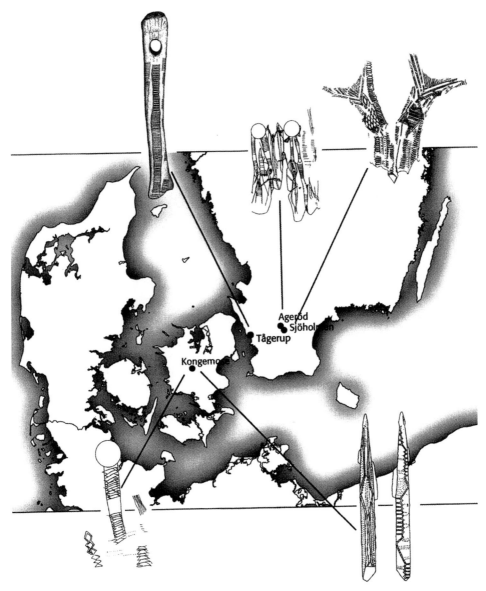

Fig. 14. Decorated bone- and antler objects from Tågerup and other sites from the Kongemose culture (Source: Karsten & Knarrström 2002).

dominated by the following; red deer, roe deer and wild boar with a small component of aurochs and elk. A small portion of the bone material shows that people also hunted grey seal at the coast.

To sum up, it seems obvious that the site was more or less permanently inhabited all year round. There are no indications of movements inland. The site with its rich evironment could be used for long periods of time.

Yngsjö and Årup

Two other sites with dwelling structures from the Kongemose Culture have been excavated at *Yngsjö* and Årup in north-eastern Scania. The first mentioned was excavated in 2006 and is located south of the river Helgeåns outlet at Yngsjö. Today the coastline is found *c.* 1 km east of the settlement. The flint assemblage is not very large and the chronology of the site is based only on the single transverse arrowhead and one oblique arrowhead. Beneath the find-bearing layer a number of post colourings indicating a hut were discovered, in total 15. A couple of these had a depth of *c.* 10–12 cm. The colourings made up an oval shaped construction that was *c.* 4 × 3 m. It has been interpreted as a dwelling. Charcoal from one of the post-holes has been radiocarbon dated to 6225–6005 cal BC (Lu S 6598 7230±60 BP). The date corresponds well with an early phase of the Kongemose Culture and with the oblique arrowhead found.

The settlement at *Årup*, outside of the municipality of Bromölla, was excavated in 2002. Here the remains of two huts or tents, workshops, fireplaces, and a lot of flint show that the settlement was rather intensively used around 6300 BC. On the highest point, 6.5–6.8 m above present sea level, signs of repeated Mesolithic habitation were evident. Later intrusions mean that the finds material from this site is rather limited. What makes it interesting though are the two huts. The northerly of these stood out as a large blackish-grey feature against the yellow sandy subsoil. In and around it 10 stake-holes, a pit and a hearth were observed. The entrance has been interpreted as being in the south-eastern part of the dwelling. Directly to the south-east of this hut lay another one of similar form. The structure was made up of eight stake-holes and a pit. A radiocarbon date places the site in the early Kongemose Culture, a little older than Yngsjö.

The Last Hunters: the Ertebølle Culture

We will begin our survey in southernmost Sweden and Denmark where we see how the Late Mesolithic Ertebølle Culture changes during this period. The Ertebølle Culture occurred throughout Southern Scandinavia with concentrations in the Swedish areas of Scania, Blekinge in the south-east and Halland to the west, as well as in Denmark and in northern Germany. The Ertebølle Culture existed between *c.* 5500 BC. and *c.* 4000 BC and went through a dynamic developmental phase during this long period of time. It is this story that follows. We can see completely new designs in material culture, like pottery, but also how cultural contacts with the continent intensified and developed during the period.

The name *Ertebølle* comes from a classic settlement in north-west Jutland in Denmark. The large shellfish banks, termed kitchen middens, could sometimes stretch for more than 100 m along the coast and were primarily characteristic of the west Danish Ertebølle Culture. One of the best studied of these sites, *Norsminde*, south of Aarhus, was in use a very long time, 5050–4050 BC. This indicates a more or less continuous settlement over a period of 1000 years. These kitchen middens are actually large rubbish dumps comprising garbage left over from meals. One interesting element in the diets of these people was the large quantities of oysters consumed. Studies of human skeletons quite clearly show that people from this period seemed to enjoy eating shellfish, fish and marine mammals.

We can have a closer look at the diet of these hunters, or maybe more accurately fishermen, based on some Danish sites at *Bjørnsholm*, close to Limfjorden in northern Jutland. Most important was eel with 56% of the catch. Saltwater fish made up 22% and freshwater fish 15%. It seems that most of the fish was caught during summer and early autumn.

At *Norsminde*, eastern Jutland, most of the catch is made up of saltwater fish like flounder with 57% of the total amount. Second is cod with 29%.

We have clear evidence that not only the coastal regions were used during this period, but also the inland regions. This is clearly evident from many areas. In the deep forests the hunters preferred red deer, especially in eastern Denmark, while on Jutland wild boar dominated.

All together, the picture clearly indicates that people used a broad spectrum of resources and ecological zones, from the fjords of Jutland to the interior of Scania. The question of how people lived during this period is a major issue though for researchers. There is no clear evidence that they actually lived at or near the kitchen middens. Apart from hearths, there is no clear evidence that houses or huts have been documented nearby. During recent years however, our picture of the settlement system of the Ertebølle Culture has changed, as will become obvious.

Recently (in 2007) excavations at the coastal site of *Asnæs* near the town of Kalundborg in western Zealand have given us a more complex picture of the procurement strategies used in the Late Mesolithic. The deep waters of the fjord and the rich seas of the Great Belt between the Baltic Sea and the Kattegat created a rich environment for Mesolithic fisher/hunter-gatherers. Radiocarbon dates document the likelihood of at least two episodes of site use *c.* 4500 BC and *c.* 4100 BC. In this context it is the faunal assemblage that is of most interest. In total, the faunal material from Asnæs Havnemark consists of 50,005 identified bones. Of these, 47,760 (95.5%) are fish, 2214 (4.4%) are mammals, 29 (0.1%) are birds. Cod clearly dominates the fish bone assemblage (86%), while roe deer account for the vast majority of the mammal remains (67%). Multiple lines of evidence, including animal behaviour patterns, indicate use of the site the whole year round. Comparisons with other Ertebølle sites in Denmark show that within almost all classes of animals exploited by Ertebølle people there is a great deal of inter-site variability. While the same animals generally occur in all assemblages, the focus of subsistence at each site represents a specialized adaptation to local conditions.

This is a very important notion that in many ways changes, as well as deepens, our understanding of the late Atlantic hunter and fishers. One recognized assumption that has been held true for a long time is that populations moved around in a seasonal pattern of settlement, from the sea shore to inland areas, and vice versa. Summer/Autumn were spent inland while winters were primarily spent along the coasts. Researchers have recently begun discussing whether people actually followed a movement pattern such as this. The material discovered at some of these inland sites like *Bökeberg* in Scania (for example bones from animals that had been hunted or fished may indicate that people lived at the inland sites more or less permanently). However, the occurrence of both fish and marine mammals at other sites, *Ringkloster* in central Jutland for example, indicates that definite contacts existed with coastal sites like Norsminde. Indirectly, these hypotheses can be supported with measurements of ^{13}C levels in both human and dog skeletons. The analysis of a canine cranium from *Bökeberg* reveals low levels, which could indicate inland settlements; however, Per Karsten also draws attention to the problems with these analyses and argues that, today, we cannot clearly find support for the hypothesis of permanent inland settlement.

In the following section some Scanian sites will be explored further.

Soldattorpet, Limhamn

We can start at the beginning. Between 1901 and 1902 Knut Kjellmark excavated a site similar to Ertebølle on Jutland at *Soldattorpet* (Limhamn) in Malmö (Kjellmark 1903). The site, and other similar ones in the vicinity, is located to an Atlantic beachridge called *Järavallen*. This is actually a beach ridge resulting from a transgression in the late Atlantic period. Kjellmark mentions that this ridge stretches over *c.* 3 km along the coast and located *c.* 200 m from the present day sea level. The height of the ridge is in this area about 5 m.

Kjellmark, who was a very prolific archaeologist, is still the only one who has had the possibility to investigate a larger part of the ridge. His observations are therefore of the utmost importance. Most important are the parts of the ridge where he identified two cultural layers with a sandy layer in between. In the bottom black layer only thick walled pottery sherds were found indicating late Ertebølle Culture activity. In the upper black layer a few thick walled sherds were found together with thin walled pottery that belong to the Funnel Beaker Culture.

There are no radiocarbon dates from this site so the date of it is not easy to evaluate. Based on the pottery in the bottom layer this ought to be placed in a late period of the Ertebølle Culture around 4600 BC.

We know of other sites with a similar context in the vicinity of Soldattorpet, such as *Nore, Gränsstigen* and *Elinelund*. They all more or less have the same figuration.

The archaeologist Anders Högberg (2002) has studied the beach ridges from another perspective and suggests that the beach ridges along the Scanian coast reveal a continuity of place, a "con-spatiality", They were used over a long period of time. Hence, the actions at the beach ridges may have varied and changed through time.

An important and often debated group of Ertebølle sites are the so-called "mixed settlements" along the beach ridges what was then the coast of Scania in southern Sweden.

Löddesborg

One such site is *Löddesborg*, on the coast of Öresund. The settlement was situated on a beach ridge at Barsebäck. The shoreline at that time was about 5 m higher than today's, and was characterized by bays and lagoons with extensive shallow areas. The site was excavated mostly during the 1960s. The excavation revealed that the site was complex, with traces of several settlements. It is clear that the location was utilized over a long succession of years, from the early Ertebølle Culture onwards. Particularly interesting is that a large amount of pottery was found, in total, 130 kg, with a clear majority from the Ertebølle Culture and only a small amount was Funnel Beaker pottery, i.e., from the Primary Early Neolithic (Fig. 15). The latter was mostly found in the upper regions of the site. The fact that both pottery types occurred together in most layers led archaeologist Kristina Jennbert (1984) to see the Funnel Beaker pottery as a part of the Ertebølle Culture, and that the introduction of an agricultural-based economy should be seen as a part of a gift-exchange system. This interpretation of the Löddesborg site led to a debate we will return to in the next chapter. There are other similar localities along Scania's coast, for example *Soldattorpet, Elinelund* (both in Malmö), *Sandskogen* (Ystad) and *Vik* (Simrishamn).

Skateholm

An important new element in the later part of the Mesolithic is that settlements are sometimes located together with grave-fields, as at *Skateholm* in southernmost Scania and *Vedbæk* outside of Copenhagen.

Skateholm (Fig. 16), which was excavated by Lund researcher Lars Larsson at the beginning of the 1980s, includes three localities with a large chronological distribution. In general, the sites Skateholm I–III extend over the entire Ertebølle Culture. Radiocarbon dating places the first site (II) in the timespan 5600–5400 BC. *Skateholm I* dates to between 5200 and 4800 BC. The youngest of these dates is also the endpoint for settlement at Skateholm I. The youngest site is *Skateholm III*. The site had been destroyed by a gravel pit, but a preserved skeleton has been dated to *c.* 4700 BC. A large number of graves have been examined at Skateholm

Skateholm I included 64 graves with a total of 63 people and seven dogs (Fig. 17), while *Skateholm II* included 22 graves and two separately buried dogs (Fig. 18). Interestingly, one of the richest graves contained a dog burial (Fig. 21). Based on preserved human skeletons, we can create a picture of how people lived as well as what they looked like. The individuals buried here reveal rather large variations in bodily constitution. Some individuals were more powerfully built, while others were more fragile. Men had an average height of 168 cm, but there were individuals who were 181 cm. Women had an average height of 155 cm, with variation between 150 and 160 cm.

Regarding average lifespan, men lived to be about 45 years old, and women, 40 years old. One large problem when estimating average lifespan is infant mortality, which we assume was high (Figs 19–20).

One important aspect at Skateholm, as well as at Vedbæk, is the combination of settlements and grave-fields, which creates the impression that this was the normal arrangement for

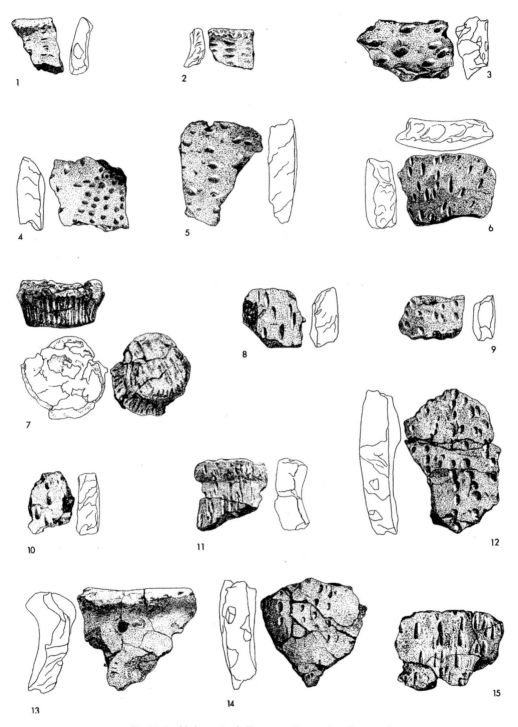

Fig. 15. Löddesborg: Ertebølle pottery (Source: Jennbert 1984).

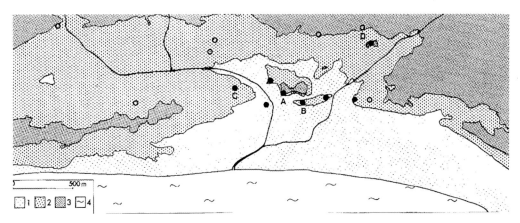

Fig. 16. Map of Skateholm and the cemeteries A. Skateholm 1, B. Skateholm 2, C. Skateholm 3 (Source: L. Larsson 1984).

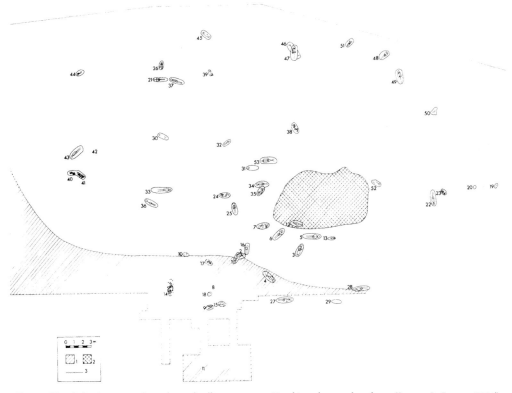

Fig. 17. Skateholm 1; crossmarking shows dwelling structure. Hatching chows culturelayer (Source: L. Larsson 1984).

the period. We are able to study changes in burial rituals, social status and health in the material found.

The most extensive analysis of Mesolithic mortuary ritual is that undertaken by Liv Nilsson-Stutz on the cemeteries of Vedbæk Bøgebakken, and Skateholm I and II. She

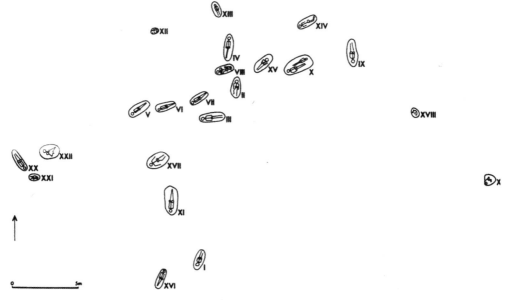

Fig. 18. Skateholm 2 (Source: L. Larsson 1984).

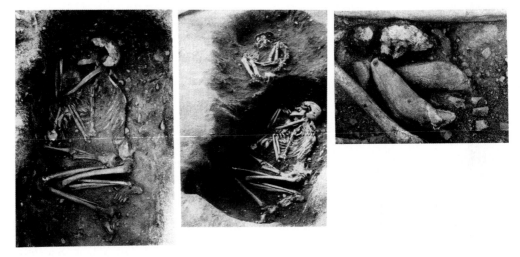

Fig. 19. Skateholm 1: Burials. Grave 41 on the left, grave 40 in the background. The child had two bear teeth on its chest (Source: Larsson 1984).

discusses the burials as the preserved material as part of a series of gestures related to the funerary process.

At Skateholm Lars Larsson has elucidated ritual activity, noting the presence of wooden structures built over graves at Skateholm I that appear to have been burned down as part of the burial ritual and a mortuary house at Skateholm II containing layers of red ochre and soot. Further evidence that fire could be an important part of the mortuary rites is provided.

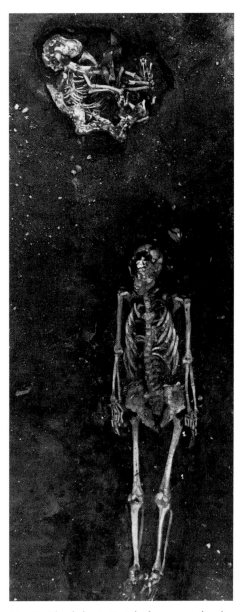

Fig. 20. Skateholm 1: Burial. Grave 14 with an elderly man and a young female on top of him (Source: L. Larsson 1984).

Fig. 21. Skateholm 1: Burial of a man and a dog. (Source: L. Larsson 1984).

What kinds of contact networks did these people have? We can see that they had contacts with groups of people on the European continent who were already farmers. These groups are often collectively labelled Linear Pottery Culture. The unfamiliar objects that turn up in Denmark and Scania may be different kinds of ground stone axes and antler axes, whose origins can be traced to central parts of Europe. As far as we can judge, the motivation to begin making pottery came from the farmers on the continent as well as perhaps from the east.

Tågerup

Houses and burials

We once more have to return to *Tågerup* in western Scania. One of the most exciting new discoveries made during later years are the houses and huts recorded in connection with the extensive archaeological excavations in the area.

House I is a circular structure and House II is a rectangular longhouse with an area of *c.* 85 m² and with a line of centrally placed posts holding up the roof. House III measures 15 × 4.5 m, with an opening towards the south. Dating of the houses is not so straightforward; it is based on flint tools such as transverse arrowheads as well as pottery found in House III. Pottery was not produced in southern Scandinavia before 4600 BC at the earliest. If this interpretation is correct, then the hut is younger than this (Figs 22–23).

Of other well preserved implements we can mention a percussion stick of antler that was placed into a 1.5 m long wooden shaft as well as a couple of *c.* 3 m long wooden spears, probably used for sea hunting.

Of the utmost interest are the inhumation burials excavated at the site. Three burials have been identified at Tågerup as belonging to the Ertebølle Culture, burials

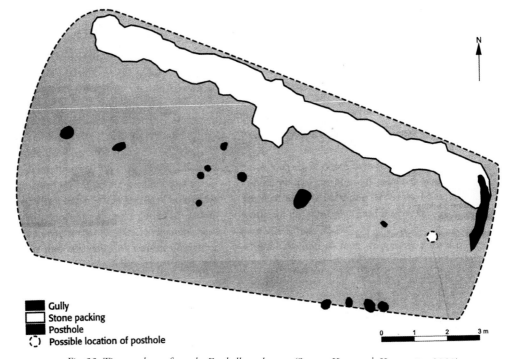

Gully
Stone packing
Posthole
Possible location of posthole

0   1   2   3 m

Fig. 22. Tågerup: house from the Ertebølle settlement (Source: Karsten & Knarrström 2003).

Fig. 23. Tågerup: reconstruction of the house (Source: Karsten & Knarrström 2003).

3, 4 and 6. Burial 3 was found in the fill of the pit containing burial 4. It consists of the poorly preserved remnants of an infant between 1 and 7 years of age, most likely 4–7 years old. Burial 4 is a rather well preserved skeleton. This individual was buried stretched out on its back. It has been determined as female. Burial 6 is a very badly preserved skeleton placed in a crouched position. It has been determined as sub-adult, 9–10 years of age.

The dating of these burials is not easy. No artefacts, except for a transverse arrowhead (Burial 6), were found. This indicates the Ertebølle Culture. Two radiocarbon dates are available but they are viewed by the excavators as being not that reliable (4932–4458 cal BC and 4906–4504 cal BC). They support an Ertebølle Culture date though.

Bredasten

Another example of a settlement with a hut structure is the round hut from *Bredasten*, outside Ystad in southern Scania. This site was excavated in 1984 as part of the large interdisciplinary project *The Cultural Landscape during 6000 Years*.

The settlement was situated on a sandy, hardly visible, ridge orientated roughly east–west. The height above sea level was up to 3.5 m with a slight lowering of the ground surface in the north-west and south-east where the height above sea level did not exceed 2 m (Fig. 24).

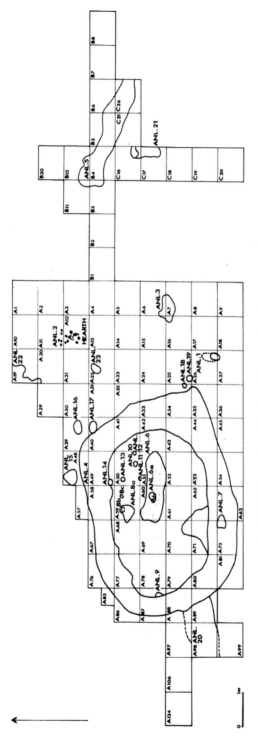

Fig. 24. Bredasten: plan of the hut and surrounding features (Source: M. Larsson 1986).

Fig. 25. Bredasten: the hut before excavation (Photo: M. Larsson).

Altogether 96 m² was excavated, probably the greater part of the original settlement. Two layers were excavated; topsoil followed by a dark occupation layer, 5–30 cm. thick. Twenty-three features were discovered, two of which were hearths, and one which has been interpreted as a dwelling. This was 6 × 6 m in size and almost oval in shape. The area enclosed by the surrounding ditch was *c.* 20 m². A number of post-discolorations were associated with the dwelling (Fig. 25).

There were many finds, *c.* 200 kg of flint in all, and much bone. Transverse arrowheads, scrapers and flake axes are the dominant types. Small transverse arrowheads of the Trylleskov type dominate the assemblage. Together with the shore displacement curve this indicates that the site should be dated to *c.* 5000 BC.

Bones of wild boar dominate the animal bone assemblage, with only a small proportion of red deer and other game. There is also slight evidence for seal hunting and fishing. The bones, together with a lot of hazelnut shells, suggest that the site should be interpreted as an autumn/winter settlement which formed part of a system of larger and smaller settlements around the then marine bay of Öja/Herrestad. At the extensive raised-beach system about 500 m south of Bredasten we have evidence of extensive sites that were used over a long period of time. Some of these must have existed at the same time as the one discussed here.

Yngsjö

The settlement at *Yngsjö*, north-eastern Scania, was excavated in 1992 and is situated close to the site discussed above. Below the plough layer a mixed culture layer was discovered. Below this was a sandy layer without any visible intrusions. The Mesolithic finds were discovered a couple of centimeters into this sandy layer. They were concentrated at a height of *c.* 3 m above sea level. In the assemblage flaxe axes and transverse arrowheads dominate. As no pottery was found the site should be dated to the pre-pottery phase of the Ertebølle Culture – about the same period as the site Bredasten discussed above.

A lot of bone was retrieved from the site. Alltogether 33 species have been noted; among them 11 types of fish, eight species of birds and 14 of mammals. Human bones were also discovered but it is hard to tell if they are destroyed Mesolithic burials or later intrusions.

3   Blekinge: New Discoveries

In the province Blekinge, the area that has seen most discussion has been the area around *Siretorp* on Listerlandet. The settlements here are located on coastal embankments and have a complex sequence of deposits. Archaeologists Axel Bagge and Knut Kjellmark conducted the most extensive studies of the area in the beginning of the 1930s. A settlement in the area called "Furet" has been much discussed. Ertebølle pottery has been found here between two strata containing Funnel Beaker pottery. This is the only evidence for such a sequence of deposits and later studies, including excavations located near the one in question, have not been able to produce any kind of similar results. It has been suggested that these results might be due to re-arrangement caused by violent storms or erosion.

There are other sites though. Over the years, beginning in the early part of the 20th century up to the present day, large scale inventories have revealed many Mesolithic sites along the rivers leading up from the Baltic into the inner parts of Southern Sweden. One such site is *Lönebostället*, situated close to the first rapids of the river Mörrumsån. The site, with remains from the Mesolithic up into the Iron Age, was excavated in 1996–7. It is situated on a sandy plateau close the shore of the river. Of finds dating to the Mesolithic we have microliths of the lanceolate type. Some of these have a distinct retouch that makes them look like barbed points from the Swedish west coast. The date of the site is difficult to pinpoint but it should be dated to *c.* 7000 BC.

Over the last couple of years though the picture of the Mesolithic in Blekinge has changed a great deal. This is due to the extensive excavations performed for the new motorway E22. The relevant part of the motorway runs, to a large extent, along the east side of a drained lake. These are the largest excavations in the province hitherto.

The development of the landscape as such, and the shore displacement curves, are very complicated and this is not the place to indulge in too much detail regarding these issues. Pollen and macrofossil analyses have indicated that parts of the area were once very close to the shore. The old lake, today drained, was called Vesan. The Vesan hollow was formed after the ice cap melted away as a strait between Listerlandet to the south-east and Ryssberget (mountain) to the west. As a result of changing sea levels Lake Vesan has undergone several changes: lake, bay, lagoon and wetland.

On the basis of the shore displacement curves and pollen analysis we have the following picture of development and changes in Lake Vesan. Only events occuring during the Mesolithic are mentioned here.

1. 9700–8700 BC: lake.
2. 8700–7900 BC: at the shore of the Ancylus Lake.

3. 7900–6600 BC: lake.
4. 6600–6000 BC: early part of the Littorina trangression.
5. 6000–4300 BC: maximum of the Littorina transgression.

In the following section some of these new sites will be discussed, starting with the oldest known site in Blekinge, *Bro (Bridge) 597* (Fig. 26).

Fig. 26. Map of the newly excavated sites in Western Blekinge. The map shows the maximum of the Litorina transgression with a sea level of about 7 m above today. From the south we have: Lussabacken, Damm 6 & Bro 597, Norrje Sunnansund & Norrje Nordansund, Norrjeskogen & Norrje cemetery, Pukaviksskogen & Gustavtorpsvägen (Source: Björk et al. 2015).

Bro 597

This site was situated at a former outlet from Lake Vesan towards the Baltic Sea. This must have been a very attractive location as there are other Mesolithic sites in the area that were similarly situated.

The stratigraphy at the site is very complex. Below the plough layer was a layer of gyttja appeared which varied between 0.1 m and 0.6 m in thickness. A sandy layer with some flint was detected beneath the gyttja. In parts of the excavated area a peaty layer with wood and bark was observed.

The most interestingly feature found during the excavation was a dwelling structure. This was situated at a small moraine outcrop, obviously close to the former outlet of Lake Vesan. The dwelling was first seen as a stonefree area with few finds. It was *c.* 3 × 4 m with a dwelling area of *c.* 10 m². The entrance was situated to the west. The remains of a hearth were found outside the north-west wall of the hut. Flint and stone was detected close to the presumed wall. This is what is generally called "a wall effect", resulting from the sweeping of debris and implements towards the walls (Fig. 27).

The finds assemblage is not large. Of the 1666 pieces of flint, most are the local Kristianstad flint and only 73 (4.4%), are senon flint (south-west Scandinavian origin). Of implements we have flake scrapers, blade scrapers, burins and seven arrowheads.

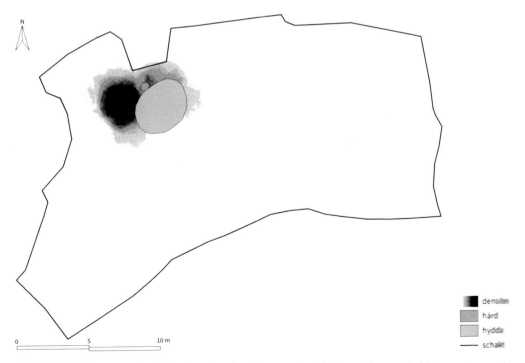

Fig. 27. Norrje Sunnansund: the hut (green) and activity areas. Black denotes the spread of flint and orange the position of the hearth (Source: Kjällquist et al. 2015).

This last group consist of tanged arrowheads, both complete and prefabricates. According to the excavators the flint material as a whole, and especially the arrowheads, have a late Palaeolithic appearance. The only datable implement from the stratigraphy mentioned above is a microlith of the so called Vig type. These are usually dated to *c.* 8500 BC.

The radiocarbon dates from the site are not of great help. They all appaear to be to young compared with the flint material. The date of the site could not be older than *c.* 9600 BC. This is based on the fact that the area was under water up to the the time when drainage of the Baltic Ice Lake at Billingen in north-western Sweden occurred. The settlement site was from the pre-Boreal period, probable the very oldest part. It should be interpreted as a short lived settlement where a group of people stayed, probably during the summer.

Damm 6

This site was situated close to that above. A similar, complex, stratigraphy as on Bro 597 was observed. At the top, a plough layer and beneath this several layers of gyttja. Thin layers of sand were observed beneath the gyttja and these were at the top of the blueish/greyish clay.

Much organic material was detected in a deeper part of the gyttja layer. Wood, hazelnuts, bark and small twigs. A couple show traces of work: a small sharpened pin and a larger stake that was worked at one end.

The worked flint was primarily detected along what has been interpreted as a shore line. The material is not large, only 1905 g. Most of the material is made up of Kristianstad flint. Diagnostic types are two lanceolate microliths and some micro-blades. Many of the finds from Damm 6 derive from occasional and repeated activities, which means that the degree of lithic variablity is low. It should perhaps be interpreted as a transit place in a larger network of settlement sites.

The dating of the site is not clear-cut. The radiocarbon dates cannot be connected with the flint artefacts, perhaps with with the exception of the oldest date of 8900–7500 cal BC (Ua-31537; 9006 ± 257 BP) so a probable date should be the early pre-Boreal *c.* 8800–8700 BC.

Norrje Sunnansund: tons of fish

Perhaps one of the most spectacular sites is *Norje Sunnansund.* This is one of very few sites in Scandinavia with well preserved organic material in the shape of bone, wood and antler. The excavated parts of the settlement were located in a *c.* 45 × 45 m area in a cultivated field. The primary area of the settlement was situated on a barely visible elevation in the southern part of the field. This area had probably been an inlet close to the then shore line. In other words, it had been coast-bound. This is something not that usual during what commonly is called the Maglemose phase. It is, in this context, well worth a mention that the settlement at Årup in north-eastern Scania it not far from Sunnansund and it is from about the same period.

The settlement was located at the mouth of a river close to one of Lake Vesan's early outlets, in an ecotonal environment with access to three different types of water body and surrounded by a pine and hazel-dominated forest. A low mountain ridge to the west added to the environmental diversity.

The settlement had been covered with a thick layer of gyttja during the Littorina transgression and the culture layer was situated between 0.7 m.a.s.l. *c.* 1 m below sea level. The gyttja layer is the reason for the excellent preservation in the oldest settlement layer.

The settlement had three layers with finds. Layer (111) contained most organic material and was a dark, humic sand layer which lay directly on top of the clay over large parts of the area. Over this layer was a layer (110) with dark, gravelly sand. There were slightly fewer find in this layer, and the preservation of organic materials was much worse. There is also a presumed refuse layer (112). This part of the layer was affected by water, which had moved the finds around.

The oldest settlement is dated to *c.* 7600–6700 BC. The younger, sandy layer, is more problematic. Based on radiocarbon dates, shore displacement curves and finds this layer ought to be dated to 6700–6600 BC. It could by no means be younger that *c.* 6100 BC as we then have a transgression.

At the settlement 73 features of different types were documented. Several have been interpreted as small, shallow pits. Other features are pin- and stake-holes, a crevice and larger pits. No hearths were found.

A concentration of 32 smaller pin- and 15 stake-holes were discovered concentrated around a crevice that was located very close to the former shore. The crevice, or gutter, measured 2.8 × 0.4 m and had been dug into the underlaying clay (Fig. 28). Interestingly, fragments of pine bark were discovered in the covering culture layer. The interpretation of this is that bark, as well as other types of organic material, was used in the fermentation process.

Excavation and analysis of the contents of the construction, combined with ethnographic analogies and modern knowledge of microbial activity has led this feature to be interpreted as a place for the fermentation of fish. The frequency of species in the gutter area is suggestive of processing taking place. The gutter contained *c.* 30,000 fish bones per m^2 mixed with the pine bark that was used in the fermentation process. Cyprinids (roach) represented around 80% of the fish found within the gutter, while perch and pike dominated the assemblage from elsewhere on the site. Roach is a small bony fish that needs some sort of preservation to be used as food.

Together with the enormous amount of fish bones, small parts of a seal cranium as well as bones of wild boar have been identified. The seal bones are particularly interesting in this context. People using the gutter probably added seal fat – not least from the brain of the seal. They are supposed to be very rich in fat.

This kind of fermentation without salt needs a rather cold climate and it is worth noticing that around 7300/7000 BC we have a turn to a notable colder climate. This was caused by large amounts of sweet water from the Canadian ice-lakes reaching the Atlantic. This obviously caused large disturbances in the flow of the Gulf Stream. So it is quite possible that this colder climate made the fermenation of fish a possibility.

When the gutter was closed and not used any more, a bone point with a decoration that is quite similar to the skeleton of a fish was placed on top of it.

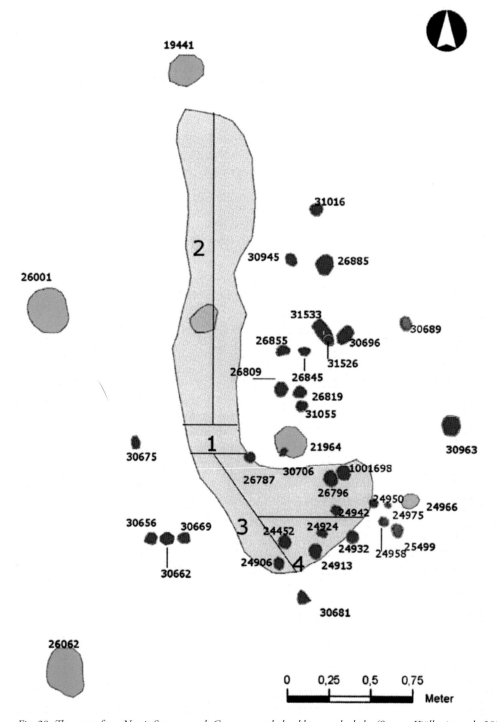

Fig. 28. The gutter from Norrje Sunnansund. Green = post-holes; blue = stake-holes (Source: Kjällquist et al. 2014).

Other features worth mentioning are three smaller areas with stake-holes that may be interpreted as huts or wind breakers; they are all a little bit suspicious though.

It is now time to have a closer look at the finds material from the site. We can start with the lithic material. This is, to a large degree (57%) made up of the local Kristianstad flint with 37% comprising south-west Scandinavian flint. Interestingly enough, for a site in Southern Sweden, a lot of worked quartz, 9 kg, was registered. Among the flint material micro-blades dominate. There are also some conical blade cores present as well as a total of 53 microliths. Most of these are lanceolates.

If we for a moment turn to the quartz material it is obvious that we have several cores present. There are both micro-blade cores and platform cores present.

Several stone axes are included in the material: in total 18. The axes vary in appearance and they do not seem to have been made at the site as there is very little debris that could have emanated from axe production.

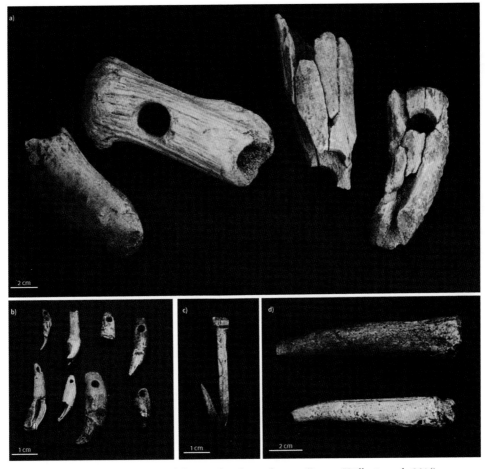

Fig. 29. Norrje Sunnansund: bone and antler implements (Source: Kjällquist et al. 2014).

The assemblage of implements of bone and antler is large for a site in the region. We have pins, needles, tooth beads, antler axes/adzes and slotted bone points (Fig. 29). Some of the last mentioned are decorated. The majority of the bone/antler implements are made of different parts of red deer. A somewhat strange find is a bead made of of resin.

Evidence for hunting and fishing is very apparent in the bone material from Sunnansund. Interestingly enough the hunting of red deer, roe deer and elk seems to be less important here compared to other sites from the same period. Fishing was clearly most prominent during the oldest part of the settlement. Very thorough analysis of the bone assemblage also shows some interesting strategical choices when it comes to hunting. Both roe and red deer are very sparsely hunted when they are young. Focus has been on adult animals. Wild boar was treated differently though. Both young and adult animals were hunted.

There is a lot of evidence for the hunting of seal. This is also unusual when compared to sites from the same period.

In the oldest layer six fragments of a human bone, probably from the same individual, were found. This is an older individual. In the younger layer nine fragments of human bone were detected. They belong to five individuals: two children, one teenager and two adults. One of them is an older individual. It is also of interest to look at the ^{13}C analysis performed. This clearly indicates that people at Norrje Sunnansund ate a lot of fresh water fish.

The site appears to have been occupied during most parts of the year, from late summer to late spring, with the majority of seasonal indicators being from the coldest part of the year. Based on various analyses it is probable that the site was inhabited during the older phase of the year by a larger group of people. This is clearly indicated by the fish storage. Large-scale food storage has been identified and implies a delayed-return subsistence strategy. The identification of a foraging economy fermenting substantial amounts of fish, and conserving it for later use and without the use of salt is of great significance. This find of the gutter has many implications for how we perceive the Early Mesolithic, suggesting semi-sedentism, technological skill and the ability to adapt rapidly to changing environments.

Lussabacken norr

Another site well worth a mention is *Lussabacken norr*. The site is situated north-west of the church at Ysane. The oldest datable finds from the excavation was a large amount of flint, mostly Kristianstad flint. The settlement was located on a bay in the former lake. It is interesting to note that a couple of dwellings were found a little bit higher up from the shore. These had obviously been used for a long period of time, and repeatedly. From the huts we have a large finds assemblage, mostly comprising south-west Scandinavian flint (senon flint). The huts are dated to *c.* 6500 BC. Below the huts, a thick layer of sand was found and beneath that a sooty, black layer in which worked Kristianstad flint was detected. This layer has been dated to *c.* 8500 BC.

4   Hunters along the Kalmar Strait and on Öland

Our journey now takes us further up along the Baltic and the area along Kalmarsund (strait) and Öland.

At the start of the 20th century the archaeologist Nils Åberg catalogued flint and stone axes from the region, Karl-Alfred Gustavsson performed intensive field surveys on both the mainland and on Öland looking for Stone Age sites. Ulf-Erik Hagberg (1979) summarized the results from these surveys, together with later investigations, in a large book about the history of Kalmar.

Before we start our discussion it is important to look briefly at shore displacement in the region, starting with the Ancylus Lake. The shore of the Ancylus Lake should be at *c.* 17.5 m.a.s.l. while the Litorina shore should be at *c.* 7 m.a.s.l.

In the early part of this century several Mesolithic settlement sites were excavated due to the construction of the E22 road south of Kalmar. From this area around 40 sites are known. They are all coastal or situated close to the coast.

Several sites were discovered in the southern part of Möre, at *Söderåkra*. The site at Söderåkra is situated *c.* 3 km from the sea and *c.* 6–15 m.a.s.l. The oldest artefacts were discovered on a sand plateau, *c.* 10 m.a.s.l. Water-patinated stone and flint tools were found here which should indicate that they be dated to *c.* 8300 BC. The excavated sites around Söderåkra are all very small and have been interpreted as seasonal sites.

The possibly oldest sites in this region have been discovered at *Ljungby* south of Kalmar. They are made up of just a few water-patinated objects. The sites were located above the trangression phase of Ancylus Lake. They could be dated to *c.* 10,000–9500 BC. It is very difficult to say something about the settlement pattern before *c.* 7300 BC. However, if there are no securely dated sites from the pre-Boreal we do have some from the Boreal. During the late Atlantic we have several large settlement sites, especially around the river mouths. The flint material is clearly dominated by Kristianstad flint, while the local raw materials are subordinate.

As mentioned above, many Mesolithic sites have been excavated here over the years and I will discuss some of these, starting with the coastal site of Tingby, west of Kalmar.

Tingby, a much discussed house

Between 1987 and 1989 the Province Museum of Kalmar performed archaeological excavations at *Tingby* about 10 km west of the city of Kalmar. During the Mesolithic the area around Kalmar was much like an archipelago with shallow bays and lagoons. During the excavations

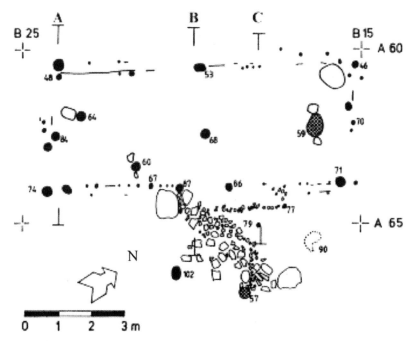

Fig. 30. *The supposed house from Tingby outside Kalmar (Source: Rajala & Westergren 1990).*

at Tingby a beach ridge was discovered that was 12.5–13 m high. At the time of the settlement we should imagine the sea level to be at this point so that it was situated between a shallow bay on one side and a lagoon on the other, with an extensive archipelago to the east (Fig. 30).

In 1987 a Mesolithic settlement that had once been located on a lagoon close to the then coast was excavated. A very widely discussed house structure *c.* 8.8 long and *c.* 3.5 m wide was found. The finds assemblage discovered inside, and around, the house was interpreted as being from the same time as the supposed house: late Boreal or early Atlantic. In 1988/9 a further concentration of Mesolithic artefacts was discovered. In connection with this, a crescent-shaped stone paving with some post-holes was interpreted as a hut. The size of the paved area was 8 × 4.3 m. In the lithic assemblage were found lanceolate microliths among other implements. Several radiocarbon dates show, however, a very large distribution over time. In this context only the Mesolithic dates will be mentioned; 6365–6130 cal BC, 5485–5305 cal BC and 5210–4970 cal BC (Ua-1316 7390±105 BP, Ua-1317 6465±105 BP, Ua-Ua-1318 6155±100 BP). The first two of these correspond very well with those from the supposed house.

A closer look at the lithic assemblage reveals that most of the material is made up of porphyrus and flint. Interestingly enough we have some microliths in the assemblage which are not that common in this region. They are clearly dominated by lanceolates (Fig. 31).

Looking further at the supposed house, we have no clear parallels for this from any area. Over the last decade more sturdy constructions have been found as at Strandvägen (Motala) and Tågerup (Scania) but they are not really comparable to Tingby.

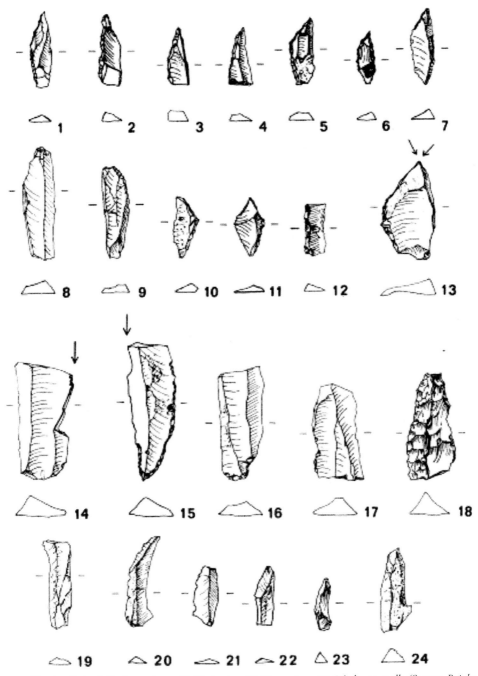

Fig. 31. Tingby: finds, 1–11: Lanceolates; 13–15: burins; 16–18: scrapers: 19–24: burin spalls (Source: Rajala & Westergren 1990).

So how should the site be dated? The lithic assemblage can be placed in the late Boreal and early Atlantic and two of the radiocarbon dates validate this; 6570–6420 cal BC and 6120–5970 cal BC (Ua-727 7650±105 BP, Ua-728 7190±110 BP). So, what about the house? The dating of the house from the excavation of 1987 has been criticised, mainly regarding whether the finds and the house were contemporaneous.

New excavations at Tingby

In September 2012 new excavations were performed, mainly with the ambition to try and solve some of the issues mentioned above. The combination of artefacts and the size of the house were never really discussed during the excavations in the late 1980s. Now there was a chance to solve at least some of the issues. In total 65 m² were excavated. Very few artefacts were recovered and they mainly consisted of waste flint material and just a couple of retouched flakes. Due to the limited scale of the excavation, we are sorry to say, we are no closer to a better understanding of the site than before.

As a final remark, I still do not see the "house" as a Mesolithic structure. There is obviously a Mesolithic settlement at Tingby but not a long house. Some of the stake-holes could very well be part of a smaller hut structure though.

Concluding remarks

During the later part of the Mesolithic, most of the objects typical for the Ertebølle Culture are absent from the area around the Kalmar Strait. One exception is the specially shaped arrowhead called the transverse arrowhead, which are commonly found at settlements on Öland and in the southern part of the Kalmarsund region but are much more uncommon in the northern parts of the region. The settlement pattern in the Kalmar Strait region is characterized by large sites rich in finds, which are near estuaries and lagoons along the coast. Archaeological investigations at *Hagbytorp* south of Kalmar indicate that the large site can be divided into several smaller settlements that gradually grew together. This is very apparent when we look closely at the distribution of the finds. At these large base sites the stone material is dominated by Kristianstad flint, a special type of flint originating from north-east Scania.

We should, in this context, also mention the site of *Lilla Mark* at Oskarshamn, located in the northern part of the Kalmar Strait region. The site was restricted to the coast and divided into three terraces. However, no chronological differences can be found between them. There are a significant number of radiocarbon dates that can help us regarding dating of the site. Dates from Terrace 1 stretch from 6000 BC to 4000 BC, which indicates the Late Mesolithic. The area was obviously visited and utilized a number of times during this long time period. It is interesting to note that flint occurs but not in the same amounts as in the southern parts of the Kalmar Strait region. The people who lived at Lilla Mark have, for the most part, relied on local rocks such as quartz and quartzite.

Öland

Intensive surveys, including field walking, during the 1990s revealed many Stone Age sites on Öland. Settlements, votive offerings and stray finds were recorded. However, very few sites have been excavated on Öland. This has, to a minor degree, changed during the last couple of years. New sites have been recorded and excavated, mainly as rescue excavations.

In the following section a couple of new sites will be discussed but the starting point is the well-known site at *Alby* on the eastern coast of the Island.

The largely unpublished material from the Alby site has long dominated discussion about settlements from this period on Öland. A large amount of material was uncovered during excavations during the 1970s where, in addition to a great deal of material from the Mesolithic, material from a later site belonging to the Primary Early Neolithic was also found. One interesting discovery was a grave containing the skeleton of a *c*. 30 year old man. The skeleton was dated to 4300–3900 cal BC (Ua-2333 5260±70 BP), which indicates the later part of the Mesolithic and would also be in agreement with the other material found at the site.

The dating of a single human mandible from *Köpingsvik* to *c*. 4400–4200 BC clearly points to the same period. One additional grave should be mentioned. During an excavation in 2007 at Tings Ene (Köpingsvik), parts of a deep settlement deposit (or culture layer, using the archaeological term) were examined, under which a grave was discovered. Unfortunately the grave was so severely damaged that it could not be dated by radiocarbon. A piece of coal from the grave has, however, been dated to 4230–3970 cal BC (Ua 34975 5255+/40 BP), which is in clear agreement with the graves mentioned above. Such a placement in time is also supported by finds of transverse arrowheads in the culture layer.

Another grave was excavated at *Övra Vannborga*, to the north of Köpingsvik, in the beginning of the 1990s. At that point in time it was dated to the Pitted Ware Culture, based on the occurrence of tooth pearls. A recently performed radiocarbon analysis shows that the skeleton is Early Mesolithic and dates to 7130–6702 cal BC. This makes it one of the oldest dated graves in Sweden.

In recent years, sites from the Late Mesolithic have also been discovered on Öland. In 2003, a culture layer about 40 cm thick was excavated in a small area at *Tingsdal* in Köping. Using radiocarbon dating as well as the occurrence of transverse arrowheads, the site can be dated to the same period as those mentioned earlier. Also worth mentioning here are the results from a small trial excavation performed in 2008 at *Skarpa Alby*, eastern Öland. No artefacts were found and the dating of the site is mainly based on radiocarbon dates from 2 features. Charcoal from a hearth was dated to the Late Mesolithic (*c*. 4400–4200 BC).

At another site, *Runsbäck*, situated on a beach ridge at 10–15 m.a.s.l, an Early Neolithic house was excavated in 2007 and 2008. In connection with the excavation, a small culture layer with pits and hearths and some objects of a Mesolithic age were found. The oldest is a lanceolate microlith that shows that the area was visited already during the Maglemose period. A radiocarbon date on hazelnut shell, produced a date of 8250–7810 cal BC (Ua-37459 8890±60 BP). Most of the datable finds, such as transverse arrowheads, belong to the Late Mesolithic.

From Öland it is not very far to the other large Island in the Baltic, Gotland.

5 Seal Hunters on Gotland

The first proper excavation of a Stone Age site on Gotland was undertaken between 1888 and 1893 at the Cave site *Stora Karlsö* (island). After that, several more sites were found on the island. The first Mesolithic site was discovered at *Svalings* and the first "*axe sites*" were discovered *Nasume* and *Tofta*. The last is important and was discovered in 1914.

The first pioneer phase on Gotland is dated to the period approximately 7400–5500 BC. The oldest sites are from the late stages of Ancylus Lake. During this time the island was smaller than it is today and contained many small lakes, thus presenting a slightly different landscape than today. The earliest inhabitants of Gotland were limited in their food resources due to a lack of larger mammals on the Island. Consequently, the hunting of seal played a significant role in the Mesolithic economy. The presence of birds, rabbits and fish in the early Holocene archaeological context demonstrate that there was some economic diversity.

From this early stage we know of a few settlements like *Strå* and *Gisslause*. We also have knowledge of some burials from the same period. In the following section these early sites and burials will be discussed.

Strå is located just west of the small town of Fårösund in the northern part of the island. The site was discovered during the exploitation of gravel. It was excavated in 1936 and 1938 by Mårten Stenberger. It was a small site with limited finds and must be interpreted as a seasonal camp for seal hunting. The site is dated to *c.* 6000 BC.

The site at *Gisslause* is located in the northern part of Gotland, not far from Strå. During the time of settlement the site was located on an esker on a peninsula, placing it between the mainland and a small island beyond the coast. The flint material is poor quality Ordovician flint and no formal implements have been found. The bone assemblage is small and includes bones from grey and ringed seals. The site is dated to *c.* 7100 BC.

Taking care of the dead

In 1953 the skeleton of a man was discovered at *Stora Bjärs*. The man was placed in a hocker (crouching) position. The skeleton showed severe damage to the right side of the skull but he had obviously survived that blow. Later, he had had his left jaw crushed and six teeth were missing. According to the analysis this was probably the cause of death. He was 35–40 years old when he died. The burial has been dated to *c.* 6000 BC. Among the grave goods were two points of red deer that have been determined as being used for flint working (Fig. 32). A fragment of a barbed bone point was also among the grave goods.

In 1939 parts of two skeletons were discovered and excavated by Mårten Stenberger at *Kams*, Lummelunda parish. They were discovered in a gravel pit. The best preserved of these had

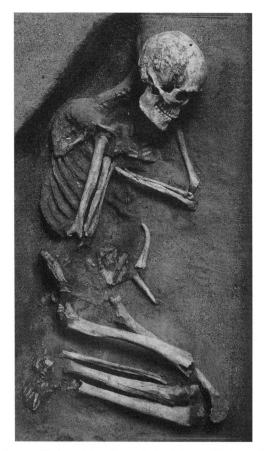

Fig. 32. The burial from Bjärs, Gotland (Photo: M. Larsson).

been placed in a crouched position in a pit. This individual was a woman of *c*. 163 cm. and has been radiocarbon dated to *c*. 7000 BC making it one of the oldest burials in Sweden. Parts of another skeleton were discovered but this had been lying on the surface for a long time.

In 1947 another excavation was performed by Greta Arwidsson. The skeleton discovered was heavily weathered but it is certain that the deceased had been placed in a pit with a diameter of about 1 m. The deceased was in a crouched position with the legs close to his upper body. In the grave, a small greenstone axe was found pressed in under the right arm, close to the ribs. Two more axes, a chisel and a axe preform were discovered in the gravel close by. It is quite possible that these were also part of the grave goods. The male individual was between 30 and 35 years of age and *c*. 163 cm tall.

The picture of the Late Mesolithic on Gotland is multifaceted. The large "axe settlements" mentioned above, at, among other places, Tofta on the western part of the island, are particularly interesting. Ground stone axes are described in the literature as being similar to Limhamn axes, a type associated with the Late Ertebølle Culture in Scania and eastern

Denmark. There is an abundance of ground stone axes, however. It is believed that the axes were intentionally left at the sites and that there is a difference between the settlements that might indicate different handicraft traditions. Settlements have also been discovered in the interior of Gotland, for example at Mölner. Strictly speaking, one cannot refer to inland regions of Gotland, since people were never far from the coast during this period.

In the next chapter we will once more cross over to the mainland and venture into the forests of inland Southern Sweden.

6   Into the Forest: Early Hunters in the Southern Swedish Interior

It is obvious that we have to see the sites discussed in this chapter in the light of the sites in northern Scania discussed earlier, like *Lärkasjöhult 4*. In the context of this, and other sites situated in the northern part of Scania, a site, *Hamneda*, in south-western Småland is of interest. The site was part of a series of large excavations undertaken in advance of the construction of a new highway in the area that began in 1992.

The site in question is situated between 15–155 m.a.s.l. in a landscape characterized by stony, gravelly moraine. Interestingly, the settlement which was 175 m^2 in area, was situated *c*. 150–200 m from the nearest water. This is a rather unusual location.

The finds assemblage is not very large and is clearly dominated by quartz. Flint makes up only 5% of the total stone material. However, by comparison *c*. 50% of identifiable implements are made of flint. In this group blades and broken micro-blades are the most common. The site is difficult to date closely and the excavator, Bo Knarrström, dates it to *c*. 7500–7000 BC. It should belong to the same period as some of the sites discussed below.

Most of the sites are, except perhaps for Hamneda, located along the waterways and lakes such as Nissan River and Lake Bolmen. Archaeologists Kjellmark, Sundelin and Lidén performed initial work in the South Swedish interior. They located several Mesolithic sites during field surveys in the early parts of the 20th century. From an archaeological perspective the area around the ancient Lake Bolmen (Fornbolmen) is very interesting. Both Kjellmark and Sundelin worked in the area in the beginning of the 20th century. Their aim was to elucidate the migration routes of early hunters into the South Swedish interior. They also located several Stone Age sites around the ancient shore of Lake Bolmen around 150 m.a.s.l.

In modern times five Mesolithic settlements close to the ancient shore of Lake Bolmen have been investigated. When the first humans came to this landscape it looked very different from what we see now. The retreating ice had left a young and instable landscape with lots of boulders. There were no peatbogs and the lakes were deep, clear and rich in nutrients,

In this context, sites like *Anderstorp* and *Forsheda* could be mentioned. They were investigated in the 1990s. These sites have all been located close to the former shore and have yielded a rich flint inventory that could be dated to around 7000 BC. No substantial remains, like dwellings, have been found at the sites though, only hearths and pits.

One of the oldest settlements is a small site excavated around 2000 (*RAÄ 71*) in the southern part of the province close to the small municipality of Markaryd. The site is interesting in several aspects, such as the small number of finds (only flint), a hut structure and a very early date of 7444–7306 cal BC. The hut was empty of any finds and was comprised a stone circle. The date corresponds well with the dating of Lärrksjöhult, mentioned above which was dated to *c.* 7500 BC.

The flint artefacts from RAÄ 71, as far as we can say, all emanate from Southern and Western Sweden. The interpretation of the site is that it was visited briefly by a small group of people who followed the River Nissan and ended up here. This site was situated only *c.* 20 km to the south-west of Hamneda.

In the beginning of this century a Mesolithic site was excavated at *Nennesmo* (Gislaveds municipality). The settlement was once situated at a peninsula along a shore. The finds assemblage is vast with close to 15,000 pieces of flint. Lanceolate microliths as well as other types of microliths are included in the material as well as both micro- and blade cores. The artefacts clearly show a close affinity to the Swedish west coast. People probably used the River Nissan to arrive at the site and also used the river for communications. The rich finds material makes an interpretation of this site a year-round settlement probable. The settlement could be dated to the Maglemose Culture.

Another site worth mentioning in this context is *Anderstorp*. The site was situated only a couple of kilometres north of Nennesmo. No features were found but close to 5000 artefacts of different types, including micro-blades and blades as well as pecked stone axes. The material is very similar to that from Nennesmo and is dated to the same period.

In 2012 The County Museum in Jönköping investigated a much larger site in *Smålandsstenar c.* 800 m from the River Nissan. About 1 km to the east of the settlement lies Lake Bolmen. The most interesting feature found was the remains of a dwelling structure. This could be classified as a sunken feature, *c.* 0.1 m deep. A hearth was discovered in the western part of the structure. Inside the dwelling most of the flint objects was found around the hearth and the entrance, in the southern part of the hut. The flint material comprised micro-blades and micro-blade cores. A radiocarbon date of *c.* 7300–6900 BC cal is in good accordance with the flint material.

7 Pioneers: Hunters in Eastern Middle Sweden

Our next stop on our journey through the Mesolithic landscape of Sweden will be Eastern Middle Sweden. For a long period of time it was believed that there had been no Stone Age population in this region. Oscar Montelius was the first archaeologist to suggest this in the early parts of the 1870s. This was primarily based on the lack of finds at that period in time.

During the international congress held in Stockholm in 1874, several finds from the Södertörn Peninsula, south of Stockholm, were presented and discussed. This obviously changed Montelius's views and he went on to discuss these later.

During the 1930s investigations were made by archaeologist Sten Florin, who laid the foundation for the models and interpretations later put forward by Stig Welinder in 1977. During this period, he excavated four sites in the area: *Sjövreten, Hagtorp, Östra Vrå* and Överåda. The last two are dated to the Neolithic. These investigations formed the basis for Welinders' discussion of the period in Eastern Middle Sweden (1977).

He defined this as the period where no farming, livestock or pottery existed. He also defined two geographic/topographic regions; Inland and Archipelago. If people had used both the Inland as well as the Archipelago this would have meant migration over more than 100 km. The area is vast. Stig Welinder put forward a hypothesis that suggests the settlement structure was based on a base camp with smaller sites used more seasonally. He also suggested that these sites had been used over a long period of time but they were moved in response to shore displacement. In 1977 Welinder, in a study about the Mesolithic in the region, suggested that there were two different groups of people in the region. These are defined by their use of stone material and named the Quartz and Flint groups. The first is seen to be a local group with no external contacts, using local raw material and pecked axes. This group is dated by Welinder to *c.* 5000–2500 BC. The Flint group, on the other hand, had external contacts with primarily the Swedish west coast. They used flint and produced micro-blades and handle cores. This group is dated to *c.* 5000–4000 BC. It is, today, very difficult to uphold this division as no "clean" settlements from either the Quartz or Flint groups have been discovered. This will become obvious in the discussion below.

Östergötland: new discoveries

Our first stop will be the province of Östergötland where many very interesting excavations over the last 20 years really have changed our notion of the Mesolithic in this region.

"At different places in Scandinavia and around the southern shores of the Baltic Sea, remains have been found of a strange, ancient culture, still essentially shrouded in mystery, a culture which in many ways bears the stamp of the Palaeolithic era and which Stjerna has therefore called the Epipalaeolithic … It is from this Epipalaeolithic culture that the first traces of human culture in Östergötland derive. They are not numerous".

This citation, taken from the Swedish archaeologist Birger Nerman, in 1912 clearly states the way that archaeologists viewed the Mesolithic at that time. Today our knowledge of this period has changed and expanded.

Until just a few decades ago, the Mesolithic was a weakly represented period in the archaeological material from Östergötland. The only finds were a small number of harpoons and points of bone and antler from the Norrköping area and around Lake Tåkern. A few settlement sites were known, such as *Åby Fyrbondegård* near Ödeshög and *Borgsmon* south of Norrköping.

In the last 15 years, however, our picture of the Mesolithic in Östergötland and, for that matter, the whole of Eastern Central Sweden, has changed. Field surveys around Lake Tåkern have yielded many new and valuable discoveries in the form of both stray finds and settlement sites. Previously, the number of sites was small and the picture of the period was vague. Now, no less than *c.* 2000 sites are known (Fig. 33).

Newly discovered settlement sites in Östergötland that may be mentioned include *Högby, Mörby, Storlyckan, Lilla Åby Kanaljorden, Strandvägen, Verkstadsvägen* (Motala) and a couple of sites from Linköping. At several of these sites, remains of post-built huts have been found, along with occupation layers and hearths. Of special interest, in this context, are the burials and votive offerings from the Motala sites.

We will begin by discussing the sites in the vicinity of the city of Mjölby: *Mörby, Högsby* and *Storlyckan*. The oldest dated house remains hitherto found in Sweden were excavated at the *Mörby* site. It is important to point out that all these sites were recorded during rescue excavations. It is not possible to discuss all of these investigations in detail here, but they are included in the interpretative discussion of man and the Mesolithic landscape later in the volume.

It is clear that the upper limit of the former Yoldia Sea created good conditions for settlement locations in later periods as well as in the Mesolithic. The oldest excavated settlement sites in Östergötland are dated to *c.* 8300–6500 cal. BC, in other words, a phase when the ice had long receded from the landscape. The Ancylus Lake at this time covered a large part of the province, forming a wide bay leading towards the present-day Lake Vättern. In the district around Linköping the former Ancylus shore is found at 75 m above current sea level.

The majority of the wetlands and shallow lakes beside which settlements were once located were established as the Yoldia Sea gradually retreated. That Mesolithic people chose to live beside shallow lakes and watercourses is evidence of a well-developed settlement strategy. The sites are in wetland zones allowing optimum utilization of resources, where different biotopes provided the basic necessary food intake. The combination of wetlands/lakes/flowing water and forest, usually with a pronounced hill close to the settlements, was crucial for the choice

Fig. 33. The Province of Östergötland, showing the Ancylus shore lines c. 75 m.a.s.l. (Source: Carlsson 2014).

of location. The wetlands and the shallow lakes, especially those lying close to the clay soils of the plains, were high in nutrients.

The Mjölby sites

Mörby

In 1996 a large area with a rich concentration of prehistoric structures was excavated in connection with motorway expansion at *Mörby* in western Östergötland. The area is bounded to the east by a moraine ridge and a steep hill, and to the west by a bog. The site is situated on a slope *c.* 125–127 m.a.s.l. The soils consist of sand beneath the topsoil. Following the removal of this by machine, dark, thick bog deposits, which are most likely the remains of an earlier lake or bog, were identified in the northern section. Within the excavation area several black strips, the remains of earlier creeks, were also identified. Between these were remains of curved sand dunes of varying size.

The quartz assemblage from Mörby is larger than the flint and includes debitage, cores and micro-blades. Without exception, the reduction of this raw material is by platform technology. The majority of this assemblage can be assigned a Mesolithic age, as indicated by the presence of conical micro-blade cores and micro-blades. An important feature of the assemblage is the use of locally available raw materials, including quartz and silicified tuff (*hälleflint*) as well as porphyric granite and metamorphic sandstone.

Of the two excavation areas (B and C) it was only at Area C where reasonably clearly defined structures could be defined. Stake-holes created two round to oval structures with openings towards the south-east (Fig. 34). These were *c.* 10 m in circumference and *c.* 6 m from each other. House I was a post-supported construction with an additional opposed opening in the south-west, away from the lake. House II was a wall trench construction with post-holes at the opening,

Both houses had solid supporting constructions, as shown by the average diameter of the stake-hole of *c.* 0.5 m, which indicate that these do not merely represent short visits to the site. Both of the houses are radiocarbon dated to the Early Mesolithic *c.* 8000–7000 cal. BC. There were no indications of floor areas in either structure and no hearths were identified either inside or directly associated with either house.

Sand covered houses: Högby

The next site of interest here is *Högby* close to Mjölby. Here a 400 m² area with features in the form of hearths, pits and post-holes was identified after the removal of the topsoil (Fig. 35). During the course of excavation it became apparent that aeolian sands had covered the site and this level was removed, partially by machine. A 0.2 m thick layer of aeolian sand overlaid additional structures, primarily in the south-western part of the excavation area.

A total of 39 structures were excavated. Stake-holes were the most common feature; however, hearths and varying forms of pits were also identified. The post-holes were found in two concentrations, one in the southern part of the excavation area, and one in the central section. Most importantly, the southern concentration had a round–oval form and was interpreted as the remains of a post-supported house structure, with an estimated diameter of *c.* 3 m. The opening of this structure faced towards the west. The northern post-hole concentration has a similar round–oval form and a diameter of up to 3.5 m, with the opening facing towards the north-west. One hearth (A12) may have been inside this building.

Hearths or hearth pits were most common in the area between the two concentrations of post-holes. In this area two areas with fire-cracked stones, that were most likely originally connected, were excavated. The structures contain a thin layer of fire-cracked stone with dark grey, sooty sand. There is clearly a connection between the houses and these structures and it is most likely that they represent expended fire-cracked stone and other refuse that has been removed from the houses.

The assemblage from the area around the house gives no clear indication of the age of the site, other than that it is most likely from the Mesolithic. In one of the radiocarbon dated pits however (A19), artefacts of both quartz and flint were found, including flint micro-blades

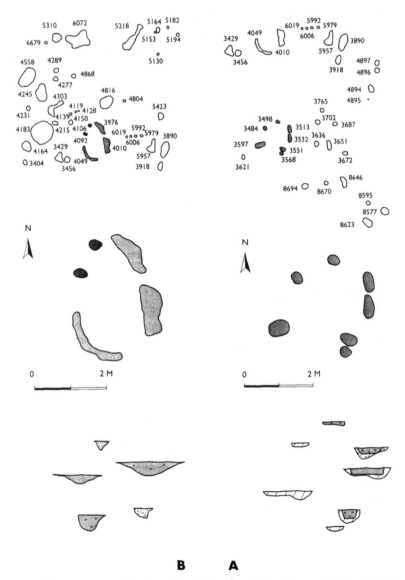

Fig. 34. The two excavated dwellings from Mörby, Östergötland (Source: Kaliff et al. 1997).

(Fig. 36). More precise indications of the age of the site are provided by the 11 radiocarbon dates, nine of which are Mesolithic. The values fall into two groups at 8100–6700 BC and 6300–5500 BC.

This dating corresponds with the pre-Boreal/Boreal periods. The youngest phase, dated to the Atlantic, is characterized by handle cores and micro-blades in soft-hammer technique. A few fragments of burnt bone have been determined as coming from beaver.

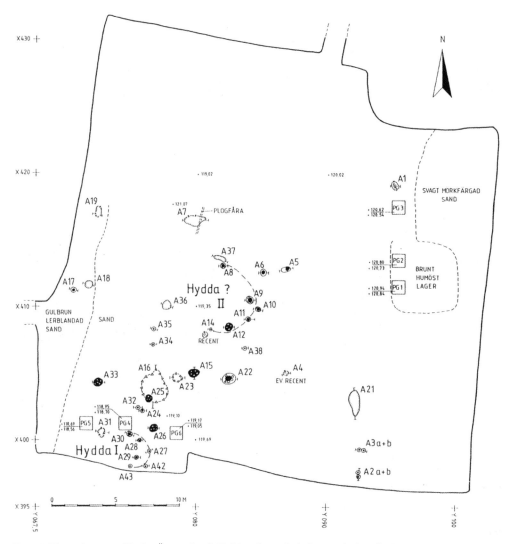

Fig. 35. The settlement at Högby, Östergötland: Hydda = hut. Black denotes the hearths (Source: M. Larsson 1996).

Three radiocarbon dates are available from the sand covered structures in the south-western part of the site. All of these fall within the oldest group. This indicates that house construction in this area of the site, together with the hearths/hearth pits, all belong to the earliest occupation phase of the site. Most likely, the fire-cracked rock concentrations also belong to this early phase. Figure 37 shows a possible reconstruction of the Mesolithic settlement.

Storlyckan: another site with a dwelling structure

The settlement site *Storlyckan* is situated in western Östergötland about 20 km from the ones discussed above. The settlement has an optimum location in a sheltered spot on a natural

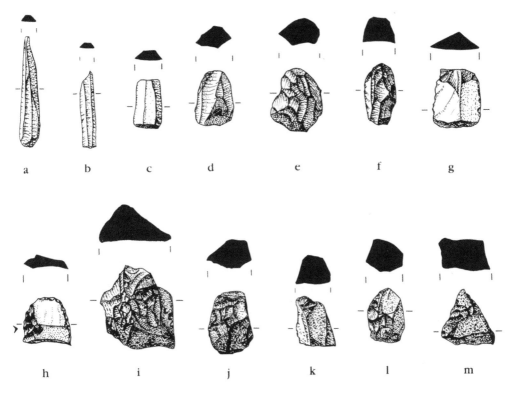

Fig. 36. Högby: some examples of finds from the site: a–c: flint micro-blades; d–l: quartz cores (Source: M. Larsson 1996).

terrace below the highest coastline, about 135 m above sea level. The terrace is naturally demarcated to the west, east and south by the swash zone of the highest coastline (the Baltic Ice Lake) and by a steep slope down towards a fen.

The hut

The stratigraphy was complex, mainly because of the nature of the subsoil. In the untouched bottom layer four distinct features were documented and excavated: a hearth pit and three stone-lined post-holes (Fig. 38). All these features were observed at a higher level in the layer but could not be fully documented until the untouched bottom layer was reached. The hearth pit was oval, measuring 1.05 × 0.70 m. A large quantity of fire-cracked stone was found in the hearth pit. The post-holes had a rounded form, 0.25–0.30 m across and 0.20–0.30 m deep. The features coincided with an area that had obviously been cleared of stones, which was mostly outlined by a number of large moraine boulders lying in a semicircle. This area was interpreted at an early stage as the site of a dwelling structure. It appeared as if stone had been thrown up against a wall which had been supported by the kerb of boulders. The hut opened to the east and here too the area seemed to have been cleared of stones. When viewed

Fig. 37. Reconstruction of the Högby site (Source: M. Larsson 1996).

in this way, the three post-holes would be the remains of the roof-supporting structure. The hut measures about 4.70 × 3.75 m, thus giving a living area of about 15 m².

About 10 m down the slope, an oval hearth pit was found, measuring 2.00 × 1.50 m and 0.30 m deep. The filling contained a large quantity of fire-cracked stone and a concentration of soot and charcoal. Close to the hearth pit was a grindstone of granite, almost rectangular, deliberately cut to shape and with a roughly ground surface.

Two Mesolithic features from this site have been radiocarbon dated. The samples are from charcoal found in hearth pits both in the hut and in the activity area with the grindstone. The charcoal comes from pine. The dates agree, placing the settlement site between 7000–6550 BC. This corresponds to the chronological placing of the artefacts, with micro-blades mainly from conical cores and small scrapers with rounded shapes. Fire-cracked stones from the hearth pit with the grindstone were dated by thermo-luminescence to 6593 ± 536 cal. BC showing good agreement with the radiocarbon dates.

The proportion of definable artefacts from the site is moderate. Apart from a large quantity of micro-blades there were, in all, 13 scrapers, eight of flint, three of quartz, and the other two of silicified tuff (*hälleflint*) The distribution of the artefacts overall is as follows: 43% are of quartz, 47% of flint, and 10% of silicified tuff. At least some of the blades originated from conical micro-blade cores. The reduction methods for quartz working represented on the site can be studied mainly from the cores and flakes. Both bipolar knapping and reduction by

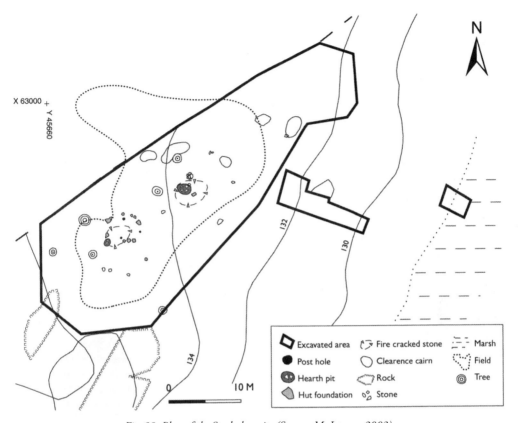

Fig. 38. Plan of the Storlyckan site (Source: M. Larsson 2003).

means of the platform method are represented. They probably represent different stages in the working of the quartz. It has previously been claimed that a bipolar reduction method occurs frequently at Mesolithic sites in Eastern Central Sweden.

Spatial distribution

The flint material is almost totally confined to the hut, and an area to the north beside the entrance. The distribution of flint cores and scrapers also agrees with this picture. The analysis of micro-debitage also shows its occurrence in the area and also outside the hut. This might support a view that waste was cleared out of the hut. The flint micro-blades, on the other hand, show a completely different picture, almost all of them being inside the hut, with a large concentration in the middle (Fig. 39).

The quartz objects were mostly found beside the hut and within an area just south of it where an anvil stone was located. The anvil stood upright. Five bipolar cores of quartz and one core of silicified tuff were scattered around the anvil stone. In addition, there was an even distribution of mainly flakes, flake fragments, and debris.

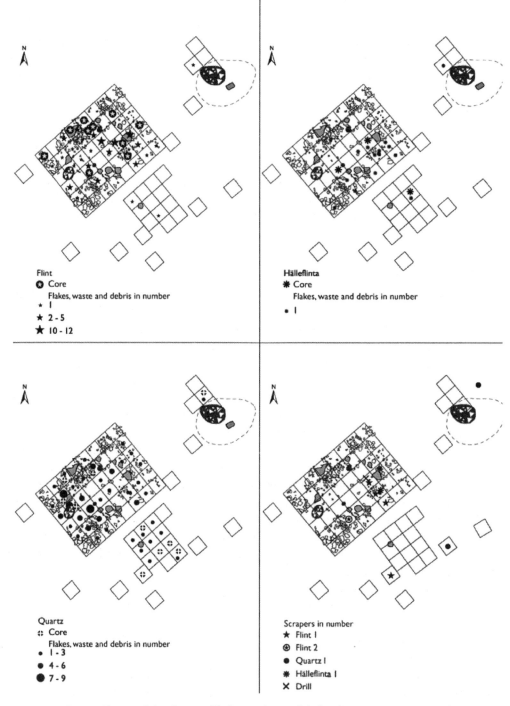

Fig. 39. The spatial distribution of finds in and around the hut (Source: M. Larsson 2003).

Western Östergötland, Lake Tåkern

Intensive field surveys during the 1970s and early 1980s by Hans Browall around Lake Tåkern has provided knowledge of some really interesting sites in that area. In this context we can mention *Holmen* close to the lake shore. Here many implements were found during field walking. Worth mentioning are stone axes of different types, a micro-blade and some antler/ bone tools – among them an antler chisel decorated with a geometric pattern. Radiocarbon dates place the site between 5600 and 4800 BC. Close by a red coloured area was found by the local farmer and excavation revealed parts of a human skull, radiocarbon dated to 5720–5580 cal BC. This is certainly the remains of a burial. Further isotopic analysis of diet demonstrated that the individual had mostly eaten food from terrestrial animals with only a minor element of fish. Another, older, burial was found among the Neolithic burials at the destroyed megalithic site at *Alvastra*. The skeleton is of a man and dates to *c.* 6300 BC. Comparing the two burials, it is interesting that isotope analysis show that the man had eaten a lot of fish supplemented with terrestrial food.

Sites around Linköping

Now, let us go a little further north to the area around Linköping. Here, on the Mesolithic mainland coast, a number of Mesolithic dwellings have been excavated in recent years. Two sites will be discussed: *Intellektet* and *Trädgårdstorpet*.

Both settlement sites are similarly located close to the former Ancylus Lake, *c.* 70–80 m.a.s.l. At Intellektet, an irregular-shaped, continuous dark discolouration was seen in the ground, measuring *c.* 4.85 × 4.40 m, at the edge of which could also be seen a number of post-holes. After the excavation was completed it became clear that the dwelling had consisted of the following features: a sunken dwelling-pit; 11 post-holes; one hearth with adjoining cooking pit; and a pit at the presumed entrance (Fig. 40). The artefacts were made of flaked quartz, flint and porphyry. The lithics found inside the dwelling were of high-quality quartz and restricted to a small area near the hearth. Charcoal from the hearth has been radiocarbon dated to 7320–7054 cal BC.

The site *Trädgårdstorpet*, situated at the shore of the Ancylus Lake at a height of *c.* 75 m.a.s.l., was excavated in 2004. The settlement zone stretches along and above the marked erosion bluff on an elongated sand plateau 10–30 m in width. Below the bluff is an extensive marsh, Kärna Mosse, that was isolated from the Ancylus Lake, but we do not know for certain for how long. On the plateau itself several features were investigated, among the most interesting being two houses.

House II was of a two-aisled type with two interior roof-supporting posts and a number of wall posts (Fig. 41). Radiocarbon dates show that the house, as well as the hearths, was in use between *c.* 7580–7350 BC. A sooty floor layer, in which most of the finds occurred, was recovered inside the house. The dimensions of the structure were 6.7 × 4.5 m. The house also contained two deep hearth pits. Finds were dominated by knapped quartz and flint. The central part of the house was distinguished by a number of flint and quartzite micro-blades and around the hearth pits were found hazelnut shells as well as bones from seal, elk, red deer and roe deer).

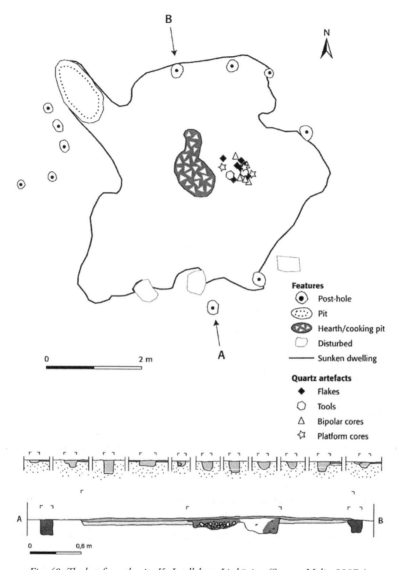

Fig. 40. *The hut from the site Kv.Intellektet, Linköping (Source: Molin 2007a).*

House I is, according to the excavator, a carbon copy of House II. This house is radiocarbon dated to 7050–6340 cal BC. most probably in the latter half of this period. The environment changed a lot between the time of House II and House I. The shoreline was displaced from *c.* 70 to 50 m.a.s.l. While House II was situated at the shoreline, House I was situated at the edge of a large wetland area (now Kärna Mosse).

Both settlements have been interpreted as being winter sites. This is based on the occurrence of large hearths and large quantities of fire-cracked stone. The robust house construction could also support this notion.

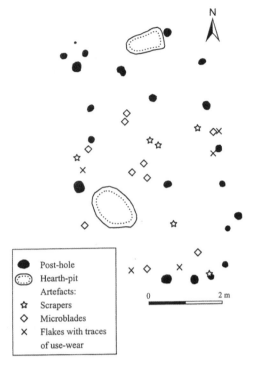

Fig. 41. The hut from Trädgårdstorpet, Linköping (Source: Molin et al. 2009).

In 2009 an archaeological excavation was performed at *St. Sjögestad*, north of Linköping. The height above sea level is *c*. 73 m in the northern part of the excavation area and *c*. 70 m in the southern part. During the excavation a small area with features was discovered. Most of these are stake-holes and a hearth. Interestingly enough the stake-holes came from a house which had two central, roof supporting posts and several smaller stake-holes that had made up the wall. The distance between the central posts was 1.9 m and the distance to the wall was 2.5–3 m. The house could estimated at being *c*. 9 m long and *c*. 4.4 m wide. The finds assemblage from the site is rather small, for example, only 57 small pieces of flint have been registered.

We have two radiocarbon dates from the house; 7040–6660 cal BC and 7320–7060 cal BC. The small amount of burned animal bones comprises only two species: elk and wild boar. This, together with the retrieved organic material, possibly indicates settlement during autumn/winter.

It is really interesting that we have three more or less contemporary settlements in the area of Linköping. At all three we have evidence for rather sturdy dwelling structures and they have similar locations; close to the shore of the Ancylus Lake at *c*. 70–75 m.a.s.l. They all seem to have been settled during autumn/winter, based on the faunal evidence. It is also worth noting that there is no evidence for fishing. However, from Trädgårdstorpet there is evidence for seal hunting. It looks like the people living here were very much orientated inland.

As an afterthought I believe that a find of a barbed point from *Lilla Åby* south of Linköping is worth a mention. The site was excavated in 1988 and was once situated close to the Ancylus Lake at 100 m.a.sl. This kind of barbed point is characteristic of the late Henbacka and Sandarna Culture on the Swedish west coast. Several radiocarbon dates place the site between 8300–6400 cal. BC.

Life and death around Motala

One of the most interesting archaeological excavations with material from the Mesolithic was performed at Motala in north-west Östergötland. Actually, it is wrong to say that it was one excavation as it was executed over many years and involved several sites from different parts of the Mesolithic.

The archaeological excavations were taking place in advance of the construction of a new railway between 1999 and 2013. Three basic sites were excavated; *Strandvägen*, *Verkstadsvägen* and *Kanaljorden*. The three sites were obviously been used over much the same period of time and should be seen as parts of a large Mesolithic settlement area and landscape. They are located only a few hundred metres apart and must clearly be understood in relation to each other, but also to the specific topographical location: the outlet of lake Vättern into Motala Ström. Lake Vättern is Scandinavia's second largest lake at 130 × 30 km and is 128 m deep. Despite its size, Vättern has only one outlet, the River Motala Ström. The group of Mesolithic sites discussed here is located just a few hundred metres downstream from the lake. The location can be considered strategic both from the point of view of communication and subsistence

During the Mesolithic the area around what today is the city of Motala was an important meeting and aggregation area. We have very early traces of settlement that show people lived here as early as more than 11,000 years ago. That is about 1000 years after the disappearance of the ice cap from the area. In those days the large Lake Vättern was a bay and further 3 km to the east there was another bay in one of the predecessors of the Baltic, the Yoldiasea. If you wanted to go north, you had to pass a narrow spit of land here. It was obviously an area of great importance. The streams and rivers were important for people in the region and acted as communicative routes. The region around the settlements had good hunting grounds, which can be seen in the rich faunal material at the sites.

Really important and interesting things started to happen, though, about 8000 years ago. Then a stream had developed that connected Lake Vättern with the bay to the east. This was, of course, due to land upheaval.

In the following account I will provide an introductionary picture to the results from the excavations. At the time of writing they have not been fully published so this text is based on preliminary results and interim publications.

Strandvägen

From the later part of the Mesolithic we have the site *Strandvägen* that was excavated between 1999 and 2003. If we turn to the lithic material, it is mainly made up of quartz and flint is in a clear minority. Very few datable artefacts have been recovered; a lanceolate microlith and a few transverse arrowheads. The first mentioned is rather early and might not belong to the main settlement. The transverse arrowheads are mostly seen as characteristic for the South Scandinavian Ertebølle Culture but also for the Early Neolithic. The radiocarbon dates indicate a rather short, intensive, period of settlement *c.* 5500–5000 BC. During this period the site had different activity areas that were spatially demarcated; cooking, lithic crafts, and axe production were all carried out in specific places.

Important items at the site are micro-blades and handle cores. These are made from three different types of lithics; flint, quartz and the matamorphic rock ultramylonite. The handle cores were introduced in southern Scandinavia around 7000 BC and seem to disappear around 5300 BC. In other parts of Scandinavia, they disappear around 4500 BC.

Worth mentioning also are the 50 or so harpoons found at the site. They have been divided into four different types: A–D. They seem, based on both typology and radiocarbon, to be of chronological significance. The oldest type is dated to 5600 BC and the younger to around 5100 BC. There are also a rather large number of stone axes at the site – 100, of which grounded stone axes form the largest portion. They are more or less polished all over the surface.

It is now time to have a closer look at the layout of the settlement. Of greatest interest here is the two houses, or huts, that were excavated (Fig. 42).

House 1

This was first seen when the covering culture layer was stripped away. There were three roof supporting posts and to the west a number of stake-holes were found that had probably been part of a wall. The size of the house was 10 × 4 m. A hearth was discerned close to a presumed opening in the wall. The building is dated by radiocarbon to 5630–5250 cal BC.

House 2

This smaller building was semi-circular or circular in shape. Five stake-holes were excavated, one of which was located in the centre of the structure. Many more finds were made in House 2 than in house 1. In this case it is interesting that a very large number of splinters from different types of lithics were found in the area outside the hut. This has led the excavator to assume that the hut was cleaned every once in a while after being used as a "stone knapping factory". This hut has been dated by radiocarbon to between 5470–4790 cal BC. It seems possible therefore, based on the dates, that the two structures overlapped in time.

Later excavations at the site have revealed more houses of the same type as House 1.

What did they eat at Strandvägen? Osteological study indicated that fish did not have an important role in the diet. If we look at other things like leister prongs and the placement of fish traps outside the settlement, however, it seems obvious that fish must have been important. The three most common terrestrial animals represented are wild boar, red deer and elk. To a much lesser degree we find smaller animals like, for example, beaver, marten and fox which are likely to have been used for their pelts rather than for food. The distance

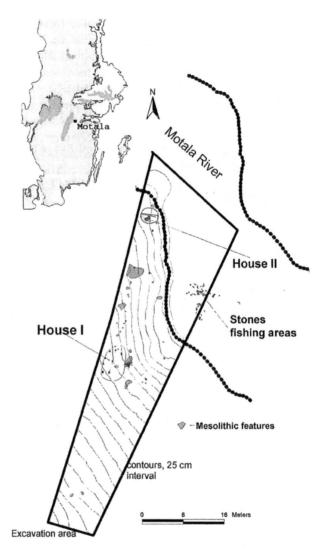

Fig. 42. Excavation plan of the site Strandvägen, Motala (Source: Carlsson 2008).

between the settlement and the salty Litorina Sea was only *c.* 30 km. In the context of the site, the short distance to the sea, streams and the lake and the lack of fish bones in the assemblage (though the material was sieved), are intriguing.

Further excavations at the site in 2010–2012 revealed the remains of several human burials. The burials on dry land are poorly preserved due to the sandy sub-soil. There is considerable variation: crouched positions, burials in pits (Fig. 43), bodies lying on their backs and even actually sitting in a pit. There are other types of burials as well though.

A low stone paving made of stones cleaned out from the settlement was found close to the shore. At this pavement some of the dead were buried together with beads of antler and bone as well as probable prestige items such as axes and harpoons.

Fig. 43. Burial from Strandvägen (Source: Carlsson 2008).

Death in the lake

We will continue our trip around Motala and the intriguing sites excavated there in recent years. In 2010 archaeological excavations at the site *Kanaljorden* unearthed a complex Mesolithic site with ceremonial deposits of human crania in a small lake (Fig. 44). The site is situated 80 m from the river and on the brink of a small lake (nowadays a peat fen). The site is a complex ancient monument that contain both settlement remains and ritual deposits from the Mesolithic. The settlement had traces of several phases of occupation preliminary dated to the Early Mesolithic (9651–8769 cal BC), the Middle Mesolithic (7030–6505 cal BC), and possibly also the Late Mesolithic although there are no radiocarbon dates from the latter period yet.

The skulls were clearly subject to complex ceremonies that involved displaying on stakes and deposition in water. The rituals were conducted on a massive (14 × 14 m) area of packed stones constructed on the bottom of a shallow lake. The stones were rather large, 50–60 cm in diameter. Besides human skulls, finds also include a smaller number of human cranial bones and bones from animals as well as artefacts of stone, wood, bone and antler.

Fig. 44. Humans skulls from the depositions at Kanaljorden, Motala (Source: Hallgren 2011).

In total, bones of ten adults and one child were found. The majority of the material comprises skulls, or parts of these. Only a few fragments of the skeletons were found. Some of the skulls have traces of deadly violence and some have wounds that obviously healed. With the help of radiocarbon assessment the depositions have been dated to 5800–5700 BC. Isotope analysis of bone and teeth show that the people deposited here may have come from what today is the province of Södermanland.

With regard to scientific results, it is interesting to mention the results of DNA analysis performed on a couple of the skeletons from Motala. It shows that the people living at Motala were not only related to the original hunter-gatherer population in western Europe but also to an unknown Siberian hunter-gatherer group. According to these results it looks like the Stone Age population derived from two different hunter-gatherer groups as well as small groups of migrating farmers from the Middle East.

Several Mesolithic cemeteries connected with contemporary settlement sites have previously been excavated and studies have dealt with questions regarding social stratification and population demographics within Mesolithic groups. However, we believe that these studies do not fully answer the question of who these people were and why they were buried there. Do the burials represent the living inhabitants of the settlement? The graves were presumably arranged to be both known and visible. Were they important to later groups of people who inhabited the site? Perhaps their presence reinforced social relations, both in life and beyond, in death. We need to consider the mirroring effect of these burials, as they become a part of the living landscape of the inhabitants of Motala.

The Late Mesolithic in Östergötland

Knowledge about the Late Mesolithic in Östergötland is still relatively poor, not the least concerning the period 4500–4000 BC. We have no large coastal settlements from this period at all. The recently studied settlement at Motala came to an apparent end before this period, at about 5000 BC. According to Tom Carlsson (2010) people's interest in the site changed. New rituals, or a changed settlement pattern, might have motivated them to move elsewhere.

In this context Hans Göransson's studies of the degree of human impact around Lake Tåkern, in the western part of the province, is of great interest. His studies clearly show that man interfered with the landscape and altered it already during the Late Mesolithic.

As mentioned above regarding Strandvägen, a broad spectrum economy, as seems to be the case, fits well with South Scandinavian evidence of a varied subsistence economy in the Late Mesolithic.

When discussing the Late Mesolithic in this region, the well-known discoveries from *Åby Fyrbondegård*, not far from Ödeshög, are of particular interest. Among other things, flake axes characteristic of the Ertebølle Culture have been found here. However, it may be that these are from the older part of the Primary Early Neolithic since a number of smaller fragments from knapped flint axes have also been found. If these actually did come from the end of the Mesolithic, it might be evidence of contacts between the people of the region and communities farther to the south.

In summary, we can say that knowledge about the younger part of the Mesolithic in Östergötland includes large gaps. This is due to many factors, such as the relationship between land/water as well as, perhaps, an earlier lack of interest in the period. Gradually, as inventories are made and new investigations conducted, these gaps will surely be filled.

Pioneering hunters: some remarks

During the Mesolithic, particularly in the Early Mesolithic, Östergötland occupied an interesting intermediate position between Southern Scandinavia and Eastern Central Sweden, where artefacts such as flake axes, harpoons of bone and antler, Limhamn axes, barbed points, handle cores, and micro-blades indicate influences and contacts with Southern and Western Sweden.

Several of the tool forms mentioned above indicate that contact channels existed between different social groups in Southern Sweden at this time. There are also clear distinguishing features between, for example, Östergötland and Southern Sweden. The most noticeable difference is that microliths are completely lacking in this part of Sweden. We have explicit evidence that, for example, micro-blades and different types of bone and antler harpoons were used, types indicating that parts of a material culture were adopted, or at least came to be accepted. Interesting observations have been made in recent years in northern Scania and southern Småland. In this area it has been possible to see how, over the course of the Early Mesolithic, people increasingly replaced flint with local raw material. The same development can be seen in Östergötland where the Mörby site, for instance, shows a wide range of local rock types. Some parts of material culture were, by all appearances, shared, such as the micro-blades, whereas others, such as microliths, may be regarded as distinguishing attributes. Differences in material culture may thus indicate the emergence of regionally developed social groups. This should, above all, be seen as a culturally conditioned group identity and not as ethnicity in the form of genetic heritage. To cite Joel Boaz (1999, 139):

> "The colonisation of new areas with which we are dealing here gradually created new constellations in which elements from the old area survived while certain other elements were reshaped to suit the new situation better. By partly changing their material culture, the newcomers created their own identity but also forged associations with what they had left behind. In other words, there is a link between the new area and the old one The first settlers in an area were confronted with a new problem: the landscape had no history or identity. New frames and reference were suddenly needed."

These first colonists mainly used flint, while quartz and other local rocks were gradually incorporated in the material culture. As time passed, the alien element, the quartz, was gradually accepted, and it also became predominant in the future centuries. The proportion of flint declined, but micro-blades span the whole time frame. We may look upon these as links with the past; in other words, they are part of social relations in the form of the exchange of goods that survived, and that developed throughout the Mesolithic.

From the part of the Early Mesolithic discussed above, a characteristic settlement form has been identified in Southern Scandinavia and adjacent areas. It comprised small habitation sites with little huts located beside lakes that were gradually being filled up with vegetation. Several such sites have been excavated in recent decades, such as *Ageröd* in Scania, *Ulkestrup* and *Lundby II* in Zealand, and *Duvensee* in Schleswig-Holstein. In a discussion of hut remains from the south Scandinavian Maglemose culture, Ole Grøn (1995) points out that the size of these huts varies, not only from site to site but also within the same site. For example, the huts from Ulkestrup I vary between roughly 8 m^2 and 18 m^2 while those from Ulkestrup II are 20–56 m^2.

There are obvious similarities between the Mesolithic huts excavated in Östergötland in recent years and the those mentioned above. They all share the round–oval shape, for instance. There are admittedly minor differences as regards the size and constructional details, but the shared features predominate. The variations in the function of the huts in relation to other activities indicate that space was arranged differently depending on where one was.

This discussion shows how difficult it is to interpret and understand traces of human activity in that the material remains found by archaeological excavation were originally created and organized by people who were steered and influenced by social and cultural norms.

The discussion above should be seen as an appendix to the chapter regarding Östergötland but also an introduction to the next chapter, about Eastern Central Sweden.

8 Pioneers in the Early Archipelagos of Eastern Middle Sweden

It is time to move along but, on this occasion, not so far, perhaps only 150 km to the north of Östergötland. We are going to have a look at the early archipelago that existed in that area and how people reacted to a new environment and landscape. This archipelago was vast and the result of shore displacement which engendered rapid changes to the landscape over the centuries. New land was constantly being formed. Intensive surveys and excavations have revealed thousands of sites from the time span *c.* 8000–4000 BC in the area that is today known as the Södertörn peninsula (Fig. 45).

We have to rely on the shore displacement curve for dating of the majority of the sites. This means that the oldest sites are situated *c.* 80 m.a.s.l. with an inidicative date of *c.* 8600–8200 cal BC. After the ice retreat some 11,500 years ago there has, on the whole, been a steady downward trend in shore displacement, creating new island-rich archipelagos on gradually lower levels. The higher the ancient shore-bound sites are situated in the present day landscape, the older they are (Fig. 46). These early sites must represent a population travelling in boats over vast areas of open sea.

The archaeologists responsible for identifying many of these new sites are Roger Wikell and Mattias Pettersson. For them, the breakthrough was a very large forest fire in the Tyresta area on Södertörn which occurred in 1999. Because of the catastrophe a *c.* 450 ha area was available for intensive surveys. The fire was deep, and because of this, large areas with mineral soil were exposed. The newly found sites clearly demonstrated that the pioneers had used even the very smallest islands. Rich marine resources must have been the prime reason why people voyaged 130 km out across the sea. The sites at *c.* 80 m.a.s.l. indicate a boat-based culture with great potential for long journeys over open sea. Furthermore, they show an early use of quartz for their lithic production. One important issue is where did they come from? The presence of the Hensbacka Culture along the Swedish west coast, with sites also inland, might be a clue. Early sites in Östergötland, as discussed above, might also indicate this. A find of a Sandarna point at *Lilla Åby* in Östergötland provides another clue.

Based on their surveys these authors have presented a model for the pioneering settlements in this area (Wikell & Pettersson 2009). The dating of the stages they define is based on the assumption that the sites were situated on the shore line and so that is the reason why the shore displacement curve is used. Wikell and Pettersson have identified four stages of the pioneering phase stretching from *c.* 8600 BC to 7200 BC. Worth noting is that Meolithic people only used quartz. In Phase 2 in particular they see the creation of larger sites on sandy

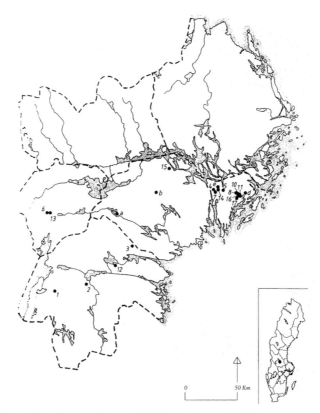

Fig. 45. Map of Sweden with Eastern Middle Sweden marked (Source: Lindgren 1997).

shores, exposed towards some smaller islands. This occurs around 7400 cal. BC., stage four, If we compare this with what happened in Phase 3, around 7200 BC, there is a marked change. The sites seem to grow larger and a year-round population is established in the region.

The period *c.* 8200–6900 cal. BC is important in this context; it is during this timespan that the archipelago of Södertörn develops into a vast world of both small islands and larger landmasses with lakes and streams. The archipelago was situated 120 km from the mainland. The landscape is young: many of the land-forms that we encounter, like eskers, smoothly polished round rocks and moraines, were created during the last ice age. Post-glacial land-upheaval is still active, creating new dry land out of the sea. In the following discussion some of these early sites will be discussed.

Early sites

Peak 85

Excavations have been carried out on the three largest of these sites in 2008–2010. The most important finds were made at a site called *Peak 85*, at 77 m.a.s.l. The most striking feature

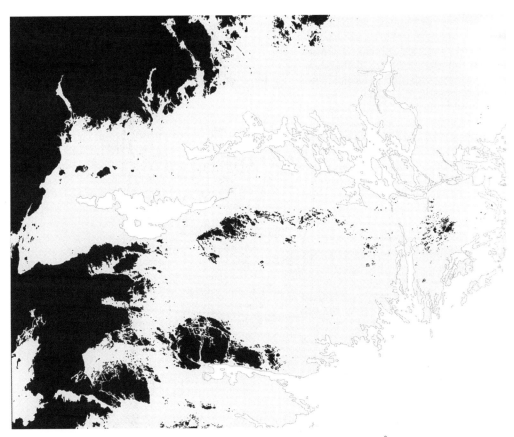

Fig. 46. Eastern Middle Sweden in Ancylus times, c. 80 m.a.s.l (Source: Åkerlund 1996).

on this site is a dwelling structure (Fig. 47). A dyke of stones fringes a stone-cleared floor, measuring *c.* 3 × 4 m. The smooth, sandy floor contrasts sharply against the overall stony moraine at the location. The stone material is totally dominated by quartz. People used a bipolar reduction method that is a trade mark of the Mesolithic in the area.

The faunal material is totally dominated by seal. Thirty-seven fragments of grey seal and one fragment of ringed seal bone have been identified. In this context the finds of black lumps of "blubber concrete", a slag-like material which is the result of heating with blubber oil, is really interesting.

Two radiocarbon dates from this have produced dates of 8205–7698 cal BC and 8246–7898 cal BC. These dates are astonishingly early and show that the pioneers established, very early on, a settlement system with base camps on the larger islands and temporal task sites for seal hunting on the outermost islands. The distance to the mainland was *c.* 150 km.

A number of archipelagic seal hunting stations have been revealed which, in terms of the small size of the occupied islands and relative isolation, were among most extreme of maritime settlements in Scandinavia during the Early Mesolithic. The finds indicate a seal

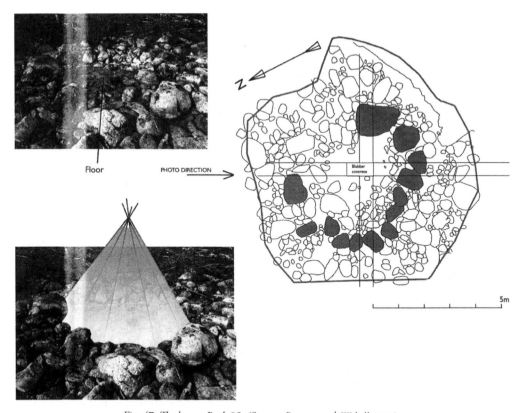

Floor   PHOTO DIRECTION →

Fig. 47. The hut at Peak 85. (Source: Pettersson & Wikell 2012).

hunting culture capable of lengthy sea voyages and of handling the logistics of hunting and camping on small and remote islands.

Sites on the A73

At about 6800 BC the Litorina Sea was at a level that is now uplifted to *c.* 50 m above sea level in the central parts of the Södertörn peninsula. In the following paragraphs a couple of the excavated sites will be briefly mentioned.

The construction of road A73 through Södermanland made it possible to analyse a transect of the landscape on levels corresponding to this early phase of habitation. The earliest of the sites to be settled was probably *Lässmyran 2*, established *c.* 6300 BC. Even though the archipelago at this stage was rather fragmented, larger islands had already formed in its northern part with the sea opening to the south-east. The site was used repeatedly until *c.* 5550 BC and, as the landscape gradually changed, the site and its shore became more sheltered by a new island emerging from the sea to the east.

Another early site worth mentioning is *Eklundshov*. In comparison to the sites mentioned above this is a very large settlement, exceeding 5000 m². The finds material is dominated by quartz, *c.* 58,000 pieces. The number of proper implements is very low. A large quantity of flake material from the manufacturing of greenstone axes is noticeable though. The features are made up of large pits and remarkably few hearths. Radiocarbon dates indicate that the site was used in two different periods, *c.* 7000 BC and 6100 BC. Eklundshov seems to be a specialized site on which contacts with other regions are visible in the form of, for example, flint.

Late sites

The period under discussion here is *c.* 5500–4000 cal. BC. We can now see substantial changes in both settlement structure and material culture. Characteristic of this period are the large numbers of pecked axes found on the settlements. Due to the effects of shore displacement it is only from this time that we can talk about a proper inland area with large land masses, lakes and streams. In the following section some Late Mesolithic sites on Södertörn will be discussed, starting with one of the sites excavated because of the roadworks on the A73. *Lisseläng 2*, situated on the southern part of an island, was settled *c.* 5300 BC. The area accessible for settlement was well protected by bedrock outcrops towards the east and west.

If this site is small, we have very large sites such as *Jordbro Industriområde*. This site is *c.* 7000 m² in area with an extensive finds assemblage. The site is situated at *c.* 45 m.a.s.l. in a small bay in the outer archipelago. Large quantities of worked quartz were found together with *c.* 50 pecked axes. The amount of flint is small though and only about 40 pieces were collected. Among these were 15 micro-blades. The features, as at Eklundshov, were dominated by 1–2 m large pits. There is evidence that these were re-dug several times. One interpretation of the site is that it was used by a large group of people for a brief period of time but, alternatively, it may have been used by a small group for a short period of time. The site has been dated by radiocarbon to *c.* 5500–4500 BC. The economy is clearly dominated by the hunting of seal together with fish and beaver.

At the sites that have been excavated, clear traces of dwellings have seldom or ever been discovered. There are, however, exceptions and one such site is *Pärlängsberget* at Järna in Södermanland. This settlement was also located on the coast during the later part of the Mesolithic. At the site, which is dated at the oldest to *c.* 4200 BC, four definite huts and one structure that might have been a hut were discovered. The huts were all approximately the same size with an inside area of 7–8 m². All were excavated with surrounding wall trenches with post-holes. It is also interesting that transverse arrowheads were discovered at this site.

Worked quartz is still dominant during the late part of the Mesolithic but the reduction method changes somewhat, from bipolar to platform technique. Christina Lindgren, who has worked a lot with stone technology, especially quartz, points to other changes in Mesolithic society after *c.* 4500 BC, such as the disappearance of pecked axes as well as micro-blades in flint. Interestingly enough though we now see the first transverse arrowheads.

After *c.* 4500 BC there are no really large settlements any more. Most are less than 1500 m² in area. The large pits disappear as well and instead we have hearths and areas with burnt stone. This could indicate a change in the settlement system after 4500 BC: It is interesting to note that, on a couple of the late sites like *Söderbytorp* and *Åby Koloniområde,* we have radiocarbon dates that indicate they were also used in the Early Neolithic.

9 Moving Inland

It is now time to leave the archipelago and move inland again. In an earlier chapter, several early inland sites in Östergötland were discussed. It is now time to move to the north-west, to the counties of Västmanland, Närke and Dalarna.

The distance from the archipelago to the inland is more than 100 km, which is quite far for a seasonal movement, so I think we have to see sites on the islands as more or less permanent, at least during the later part of the Mesolithic. The inland sites are different though. We obviously see more of the "flint group" inland in comparison with the "quartz group". Inland we also have proper dwelling structures that indicate a great difference compared to the archipelago.

During the last decade or so, several Mesolithic sites have been excavated in the province of Närke. Most of these are small and located at the former shore. The region is limited by what is usually called the highest coastline (HK) meaning the limit of the Baltic Ice Lake around 8000 BC. Mountains like Tiveden, at 136 m.a.s.l, Kilsbergen, at 160 m.a.s.l. and Grythyttan, at 180 m.a.s.l.form a kind of barrier and frontier for the area.

Sites like *Kuphälla, Skumparberget* and *Lysinge* are sites woth a mention. The first of these was excavated in 1998 and has been interpreted as a small, seasonal hunting station. It is situated *c.* 70 m above sea level. The landscape surrounding the site was made up of small islands with the mainland to the west. The finds material is totally dominated by quartz. Two periods of settlement have been discerned: around 5200 BC and 4000 BC.

Skumparberget was excavated in 1995 and was once situated in a marine landscape but today is at *c.* 55 m.a.s.l. The site has, like Kuphälla, been interpreted as a hunting station. Interestingly enough micro-blades and cores have been found, both in quartz and silicified tuff (*hälleflint*). With the help of radiocarbon the site has been dated to *c.* 5300 BC.

The sites at *Lysinge* have also been interpreted in the same way as the two mentioned above. There are differences though as, on Lysinge I, two possible dwelling structures have been found as well as work floors, cooking pits and hearths. The finds assembage is made up of quartz, flint and porphyry as well as slate. A quartz quarrying site has been indentified close to the settlement. This could have had a profound impact on the settlement. The site is dated by radiocarbon to *c.* 5400–5000 BC. As yet we have no really early dates from this region as they all seem to belong to the Late Mesolithic, *c.* 5500–4000 BC.

10   The Western Part of Sweden

In this chapter we will move to the other side of Sweden, to the west coast and the provinces of Halland and Bohuslän. However, before I continue with the chronology, sites and settlement structure a brief history of research is necessary to understand to complexity of the situation on the Swedish west coast.

The first Stone Age sites in the Gothenburg area were discussed by Malm at a conference in Newcastle as early as 1863. These sites were located at the island of Hissingen in Gothenburg and were identified by the presence of worked flint. During the early part of the 20th century important works were performed by the students sent out by Knut Stjerna from Uppsala. Their aim was to identify and register prehistoric sites in most parts of Sweden. On the west coast, this resulted in a dissertation by Enqvist regarding the stone age settlements on the islands of Orust and Tjörn, published in 1922.

In 1915 the so-called "Gothenburg Inventory" began. This is one of the most important events in the archaeology of the Swedish west coast. Georg Sarauw and Johan Alin instigated the Inventory. Sarauw was Danish and responsible for the eponymous excavations at the Maglemose site Mullerup on Zealand. He was also a botanist as well as educated in forestry. This background had a large impact on his archaeological work. Alin was a teacher and a keen amateur archaeologist. Their work was published in *Götaälvområdets fornminnen* in 1923. It was authored by both of them but Alin wrote about the Stone Age. He divided Mesolithic sites into two groups; Ertebølle and Lihult. No earlier, that is, Maglemose sites, had yet been discovered in the region.

This book became a sort of bible for the archaeology of Western Sweden. Then, in 1934, came a large publication of the excavations at the eponymous site *Sandarna* in Gothenburg (Alin *et al.* 1934). This is still the largest excavation of a Stone Age site in Gothenburg. This was followed by Alins publication in 1935 of *Rottjärnslid* in Bohuslän. This was also the first excavated site in the region with organic material. It was also the first excavated kitchen midden in Bohulän. The importance of theses sites cannot be over-estimated.

In 1953 Åke Fredsjö published his thesis on the older Stone Age in Western Sweden. In his thesis he suggested a revised divison of the Mesolithic of the region into three groups *Hensbacka*, *Sandarna* and *Lihult*. These are still used today. His main issue was that the sites were shore-bound and that the higher the location, the older the site must be. In 1965 material from the site *Hensbacka* was published by Nicklasson. This, together with *Bua Västergård*, is one of the most important sites in the region.

In 1972 two studies were published that took very different stances. One of these was written by Carl Cullberg and concerned the Mesolithic of Western Sweden. His results supported Fredsjö's to a large degree, but the chronology was revised due to the availability of radiocarbon dates. Stig Welinder from Lund debated the chronology with Cullberg and suggested three groups: the Flake axe group (Hensbacka), the Early Post-glacial group (Sandarna) and the Lihult group. The central problem was the flake axes. These were meant to belong to the later Mesolithic in Scania and Denmark and not to the Boreal or even pre-Boreal. This assumption was wrong, however, because early sites with flake axes have been excavated in both Scania and Denmark. We can, for example, mention the Barmose site on Zealand which is very early, dated to the pre-Boreal. Karl Göran Sjögren (1991) is, for example, of the opinion that flake axes were produced during the whole of the Mesolithic period. Today this is the only plausible explanation.

The earliest sites

The late glacial period is characterized by a receding ice cap. The central part of the province of Halland was free from the ice around 13,500 years ago. One of the oldest sites is called *Skatmossen* and today is situated 65 m above the sea level. This is remarkable as the highest coastline is around 70 m.a.s.l. The site dates to around 11,000 BC and was, at that time, situated on an island. The flint material from the site is made up of both blades and waste. Burin-like implements are present that are somewhat similar to the Zinken found on Ahrensburg sites in both Germany and Denmark.

Similar sites are *Spannarp* (Halland) and *Kållered*, south of Gothenburg. The last mentioned should be dated to around 9,000 BC and was situated on a small island. The artefacts were recovered within sand and gravel deposits. This site had obviously been transgressed. This site could be characterized as a flint reduction site, actually three sites, for the manufacturing of flint implements. Immediately north of the reduction area was found an arrowhead that is characteristic of the Ahrensburg Culture. These sites are not easy to date, but they are obviously earlier than the pre-Boreal period.

In 2002 a site called *Trollåsen* in Askim parish, south of Gothenburg, was excavated. An excavation a couple of years earlier had resulted in a rather small finds assemblage comprising mostly water swelled flint imbedded in deposits resulting from a transgression that had occurred shortly after it was inhabited. This layer could be dated to about 12,000 B.P. The 2002 excavation covered an area of about 100 × 100 m. The evidence indicated that a small group of people were resident for a short period of time in a sheltered bay on an island in the outer archipelago to hunt seal and fish. The soil at the site was sandy/gravelly and features were cooking pits, hearths and stake-holesthough it is clear that the cooking pits are much younger and date to the pre-Roman Iron Age. The flint material was sparse but included burins, borers and a couple of barbed points. These are very similar to those found later in the Hensbacka Culture. The dating is the same as from the earlier excavation.

Hensbacka Culture

I will begin the discussion of the Early Mesolithic on the West Coast with the pre-Boreal period. In this region, the dominating culture group has been named *Hensbacka Culture*, *c.* 9500–8000 BC. This is named after a site located in the inner part of Saltkällefjorden. The site is today situated at *c.* 65–90 m above the sea but at the time of its occupation the sea reached into Lake Vänern.

The assemblages from these sites are quite similar. Characteristic artefacts are tanged points, simple lanceolates, single edged, broad rhombic and Högnipen points, burins and flake axes (Fig. 48). The blade cores are usually conical or unifacial.

Probably the oldest site in the region, *Kvisljungeby*, was located on the island of Hissingen. It was excavated in 2000. Height above sea level is today 36 m and, together with the flint inventory, it should be dated to the oldest part of the Hensbacka Culture *c.* 9500 BC. The site is small and with no traces of dwellings or culture layer. The location of the site would have made it very exposed to the open sea. The people living here must, therefore, have had

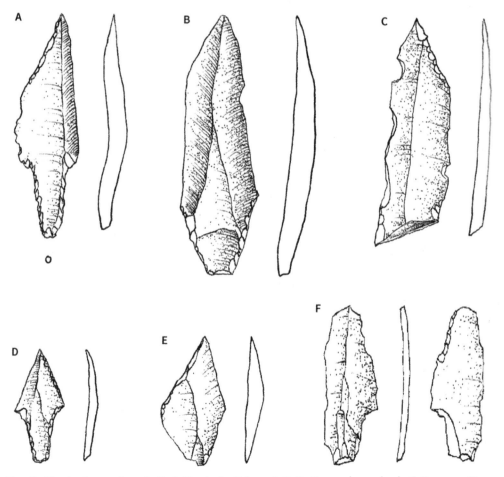

Fig. 48. *Flint implements from the Early Hensbacka Culture: A, B, D, E: tanged arrowheads; C, F: scrapers (Source: Nordqvist 1999).*

the sea as a primary source of food. Two small areas with charcoal have been interpreted as hearths. The site yielded a rather large collection of flint material with flake axes, tanged arrowheads and Högnipen points.

Another site in the area worth a mention in this context is *Glimsås* on Orust. This site is located on what was an island in the outermost part of the Bohulän skerries. The site was quite small, 15 × 10 m. The artefacts were found under a thin layer of sand. The flint assemblage is typical for the early stage of the Hensbacka Culture with, for example, tanged points and lanceolates. No organic material was preserved and the dating to *c.* 9000 BC is based on the shore displacement curve.

The Hensbacka Culture is actually made up of two quite distinct groups. Tanged arrowheads, similar to the ones found in the Ahrensburg Culture, characterize the first one *c.* 9500 BC. Everything points to this stage being seen as a local variation of the Ahrensburg. The younger group is characterized by, for example, flake axes, lanceolate microliths with pointed retouch and Högnipen points. The last of these gets its name from a site in south-eastern Norway. We also have micro-burins and bipolar blade cores. This stage is radiocarbon dated to *c.* 9000–8500 BC.

In the Hensbacka Culture we could, according to Johan Wigforss (Wigforss *et al.* 1983, 8 ff), see the following characteristics:

1. The sites are located in the outer archipelago;
2. They are very small;
3. No obvious culture layers can be identified;
4. Work areas for flint can often be identified on the settlement.

Inland sites

Do we, then, have any inland settlements in this region from the pre-Boreal/Boreal period? There are some. One of them is a site called *Almeö* close to Lake Hornborgasjön in Västergötland. The flint material comprises lanceolates, flake axes and core axes. Bone from fish like pike and perch as well as from terrestrial animals like elk, wild boar, aurochs and beaver have been found at the site. An unusual feature is three obviously deliberately buried dogs, one of which was covered with a layer of red ochre. The site is radiocarbon dated to *c.* 8300–8000 BC.

Another quite different possible burial was discovered in 1994 at *Bredgård*, close to the city of Ulricehamn in Västergötland. The skeleton was found in a bog. With the help of radiocarbon it has been possible to date the remains to around 7800 BC. This is from about the same time as the human remains found at Huseby Klev and makes it one of the oldest in Scandinavia. A thorough analysis of the remains makes it possible to identify the individual as a male. How the man ended up in the lake is hard to interpret. It might have been a burial in a canoe or an accidental drowning. It is interesting to note though that, based on ^{13}C analysis, this individual had only eaten meat from terrestrial animals. We might see this as a dichotomy between living at the sea and living inland.

Sandarna Culture

During the Boreal, *c.* 8500 BC, the climate got better over time and this had, of course, a marked impact on the vegetation. From a forest dominated by pine and hazel we now can see the development of a broad-leaved forest with elm, oak and lime. There is also a marked change in the relation between land and sea. After a long period of land upheaval we now see a different picture; the sea rises. As a result of this we now have what could be called submerged sites. Sites at the then coast have been imbedded in sand and clay and the primary settlement areas have been more or less destroyed or damaged. This is a situation that begins around 9000 BC and ends around 7000 BC. This is a geological phenomenon characteristic of the Gothenburg area as well as parts of the coastline north and south.

As mentioned above, the first site of this kind, *Sandarna*, in Gothenburg, was published in 1934 (Alin *et al.* 1934). This is also the name given to this group of sites. In the Gothenburg region all sites that are dated to a period before 6000 BC and located at a height of between 15 and 23 m.a.s.l. have been affected by transgressions. Most dates are based on the shore displacement curve for the region. Because of this, as we will see, the preservation of organic material is astoundingly good. In Scania and Denmark this period is synonymous with the Maglemose Culture.

There is also a very marked change in the flint assemblage in the early Sandarna phase compared the late Hensbacka phase. In the early part of the Sandarna phase there are core axes, Sandarna axes and round-butted axes (Fig. 49). The common points include barbed points and lanceolates. During this early stage micro-blade technology is also introduced which means that barbed points eventually disappear.

Over the last decades several submerged sites have been excavated in Western Sweden. some examples of this category follow.

The eponymous site *Bua Västergård* in Gothenburg was excavated in the early 1970s. The site is dated to between *c.* 7500 and 6500 BC. A very large animal bone assemblage was recovered with many species represented: ten of mammals, four of birds and four of fish. The amount of fish bone was especially large. According to the excavator, Johan Wigforss, they must have been really good fishermen as evidenced by an abundance of bones from cod and ling. Fishing seems to have been most important but this was supplemented by the hunting of red deer, roe deer and wild boar.

The site *Balltorp*, close to Mölndal (Fig. 50), is situated only 5 km to the east of Bua Västergård and has been excavated several times and I will in the discuss the site in more detail, starting with Bengt Nordqvist's excavation in 1987 and 1988.

The settlement was situated on a north-westerly slope towards the bottom of a large valley, directly north of Gothenburg. The lowest lying parts of the settlement were covered with clay. Several layers were detected and it was obvious that the site had been affected by both transgressions and regressions over several thousand years. Further up the slope the deposits changed towards sand and gravel. Only one feature was discovered and this was a hearth that was found at the bottom of the stratigraphic sequence.

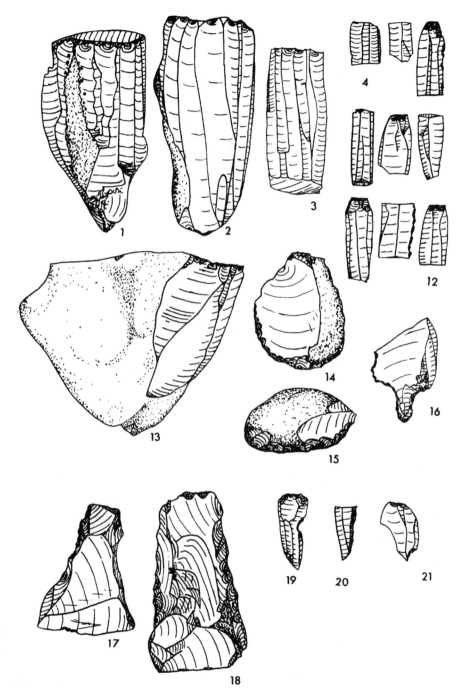

Fig. 49. Flint implements from the Sandarna Culture: 1–3, 13: cores; 4–12: micro-blades; 14–15: scrapers; 16: tanged arrowhead; 17–18: flake axes; 19–21 burins (Source: Nordqvist 2000).

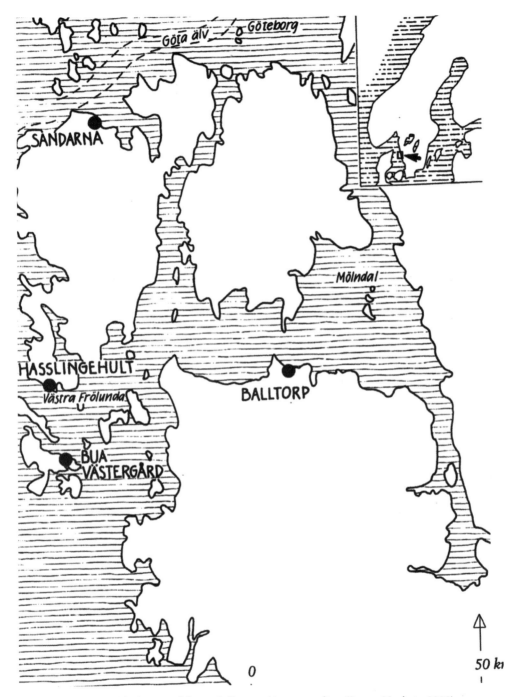

Fig. 50. The location of the site Balltorp and its surroundings (Source: Nordqvist 2000).

The finds material is rich and we have lanceolates as well as barbed points together with Sandarna axes but only one flake axe (Fig. 51).

There are several radiocarbon dates available from the site but, as usual, the dates could be subjected to source criticism. The excavator, Bengt Nordqvist, points to the fact that more

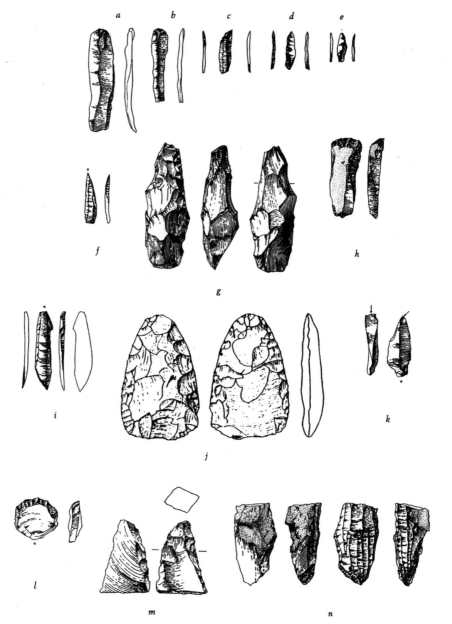

Fig. 51. Flint implements from Balltorp: a–e: micro-blades; f: lanceolate; g: core axes; i: barbed point; j: Sandarna axe; k: burin; l: scraper; m: flake axe; n: blade cores (Source: Nordqvist 2000).

dates could have been obtained and that only one structure, the hearth at the bottom of the sequence, was dated – to *c.* 7300 BC. This is one of the oldest dates from the site. The oldest date is *c.* 8300 BC and eminates from a layer with gravel. To summarize, we can say that Balltorp could be dated to between *c.* 8300 and 6100 BC.

At Balltorp, a lot of both burned and unburned bone was recovered. This is not very common at sites at the west coast. It is interesting to note that people living at the site did not utilize the abundant marine resources very much. The clear majority of the bones are from red deer, wild boar, aurochs and roe deer. The site at Balltorp was, according to the excavator Bengt Nordqvist, inhabited during the autumn and winter periods.

Further excavations at the site were performed in 1999 and 2011. The 2011 excavation involved a large area of *c.* 5000 m². The height above sea level was 15–20 m. Eight layers were documented and layer 7 was made up of sandy gyttja containing worked flint. With the help of the shore displacement curve this layer be dated to between 10,100 to 9850 BP.

The finds assemblage is rather small comprising 4000 items. This is made up of bone, wood, antler, resin and seeds as well a piece of cord made of plant fibre.

A closer look at the flint material makes it obvious that most of the characteristic implements of the Sandana Culture are present. We have axes, microliths, lanceolates, scrapers, borers and a single burin. The finds assemblage is in many aspects, of course, quite similar to the material recovered in the 1987/8 excavation. Among the bone and antler material there are several pieces with traces of working. Of special interest is an axe made of antler. It is 210 mm long and has a diameter of 4.5 mm at the thickest part. This part of the axe is damaged but there ought to have been a socket here. There are traces of cut decoration in the shape of lines.

The osteological material is very rich. We have fish, fox, seal, roe deer, wild boar and several small animals. Especially frequent are bones from different birds and interestingly, we have a rare species in the material, pelican. This is one of only very few that have been found at this early date.

The radiocarbon dates place layer 7 with the artefacts between *c.* 8400 and 8000 BC. This corresponds well with the oldest dates from 1987/8. This is a rather tight time span and unusual for the Mesolithic.

Huseby klev is another site worth discussing. It was located on what was once a small island close to the mouth of a brook. Three different sites were excavated here in the early 1990s. The first, discussed here, was named "The deep pit" and it was covered with about 2 m of clay and sand deposits. The site belongs to the end of the Hensbacka and beginning of the Sandarna Cultures, that is, the late pre-Boreal and early Boreal, *c.* 8200–7600 BC. In the settlement layer a lot of bark, hazelnuts and branches were found as well as a couple of 1 m long stakes. The stakes could perhaps have been parts of a dwelling structure. Many bone from different animals occurred in this layer. Red deer and wild boar have been identified but most interesting are the bones from seal, porpoise and dolphin. According to the excavator, Bengt Nordqvist, the bones of dolphins were found in a very limited area. This has been interpreted as a butchering area. Human bones have also been retrieved. It is, however, difficult to say that they are from destroyed burials. It is interesting to note that measurements of ¹³C from the human remains indicate that they mostly ate marine food. This is strange, as more than half of the animal bones at the site are from terrestrial animals.

Among the finds material from "the deep pit" we find, for example, fishing hooks and antler axes. One of the most unexpected finds was a rich and varied collection of pieces of resin. Almost a hundred clumps were recovered. Of the pieces ten had impressions of human teeth – evidence for Mesolithic chewing gums. Worked resin was also found. These are thin, flat pieces and some even have cord impressions. They might have been used for boats as caulking. There was an unusually rich botanical component: apples, wild briar, blackthorn and bird cherry and most commonly, thousands of hazelnut shells.

The upper layer at Huseby klev is dated to the later part of the Sandarna culture, *c.* 7500–6900 BC. The flint material is scarce and limited to a few lanceolate microliths, barbed points and a core axe. The much larger assemblage of bone and antler includes antler axes, pick axes and fishing hooks (Fig. 52).

There is also a large faunal assemblage, especially from fish. In this category the dominant species is ling. Worth mention, of course, are the human bones. These include bones and

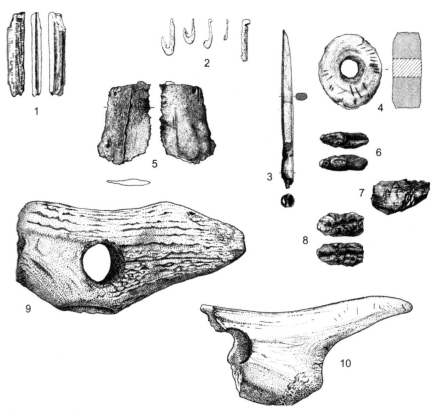

Fig. 52. Bone, antler and resin from Huseby Klev: 1: decorated slotted bone point; 2: fishing hooks; 3: bone points with resin; 4: worked dolphin vertebrae; 5: resin; 6–8: "chewing gum" of resin; 9: antler axe; 10: antler pick axe (Source: Nordqvist 1997).

teeth from at least ten different individuals. According to Bengt Nordqvist (2005) these could be from disturbed graves.

An interesting site with a dwelling structure was excavated in 1997 at *Timmerås* in the central part of Bohuslän. The site was situated on a 50 × 20 m large terrace at the foot of a rather steep mountain. In the Mesolithic the area where the site was located could be described as an inner archipelago. The site had been on a rather large island and shore-bound, but close to the mainland. When the topsoil was removed, an up to 35 cm thick occupation layer was found covering an area of *c.* 200 m². An even darker layer was observed in the centre of the occupation layer. This was the top of a sunken dwelling (Fig. 53). Around the border of the dwelling small patches of discolouration were found but it was difficult to determine if they were actual stake-holes or not. At the bottom of the depression, however, there were definite stake-holes. The dwelling is interpreted as having been a tent like structure covered with branches and one or more layers of bark with a central fireplace. The site has been interpreted as a winter dwelling for a small unit of people.

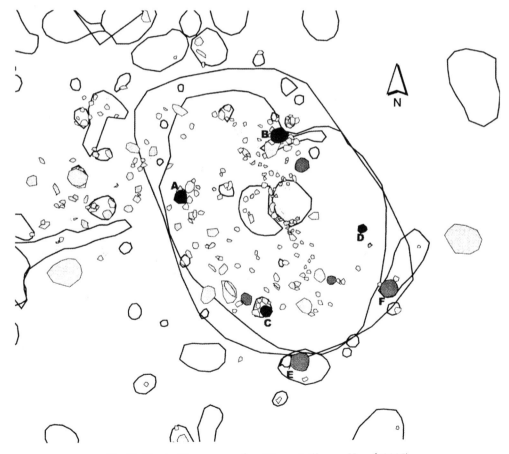

Fig. 53. The dwelling structure from Timmerås (Source: Hernek 2005).

The finds from the dwelling are made up of blades and micro-blades and they mainly derive from one-sided cores with a single platform. There are no microliths and the most common tools are small burins made on flakes. The dating of the dwelling is based on radiocarbon dates which indicate a timespan of *c.* 7400–7000 BC, that is, a late part of the Sandarna Culture.

Another site with dwelling structures worth a mention is *Gothenburg 330*, excavated in 2010. The site is on the island of Hissingen in the north-western part of Gothenburg, at 20–29 m above the sea level today. In this context only the oldest one of two possible dwellings will be discussed. This was found beneath a Late Mesolithic structure. The shape of this dwelling is slightly round with four roof-supporting posts and it has an area of *c.* 11 m². The flint material mostly emanates from the floor layer in the dwelling and is characteristic of the Sandarna Culture. Microliths, burins, core axes, scrapers and many cores were recovered. There are no radiocarbon dates from the dwelling itself but one from a hearth close by provided a date of *c.* 6600 BC.

The dead

So far, I have not mentioned any burials, with the possible exception of Huseby klev. There are very few. Diggers in a shellbank at *Österöd* in central Bohulän found one as early as 1903. It was, however, actually recovered in 1933 by Johan Alin. In 2007 radiocarbon analysis of a tooth from the skeleton produced a date of *c.* 8200 BC, making it one of the oldest known from Scandinavia. Osteological determinations show that the bones are from a woman of old age, at least 60 and probably 84–88 years old. Her stature can be estimated to about 170 cm. Although the bones are fragmented, all body parts are represented, and the body was most likely intact when interred. We interpret the find as a grave, with burial possibly having been made in a sitting position. Interestingly, the ^{13}C value (−18.0‰) indicates only a moderate intake of marine protein, in spite of the location of the site in a highly marine environment.

Another burial site worth mentioning is *Uleberg* i in northern Bohhuslän. The site was discovered as early as 1929 and investigated during the following years. It is a burial of the rather poorly preserved remains of two individuals. They were in a seated crouched position. The remains are from a man and a woman(?), both young adults. Two radiocarbon dates indicate burial at around 5600 for both individuals.

The ^{13}C values, which say a lot about the diet of the people living at these sites differ considerably from site to site and this could indicate that Mesolithic populations did not undertake seasonal movements between the coast and inland. It seems that some coastal populations had a more varied diet, eating both marine and terrestrial food. It is, for example, interesting to note the very different food strategy evident between the sites Balltorp and Bua Västergåd. The distance between the two contemporaneous sites is only *c.* 5 km but the animalbone assemblages indicate that they chose very different food procurement strategies. At Balltorp there is a dominance of terrestrial animals while at Bua Västergård there is a dominance of marine resources.

The Late Mesolithic

Lihult

The last period to be discussed here is the Atlantic and the *Lihult* phase and the slightly younger settlements with *transverse arrowheads*. The settlement that has given name to this phase is situated by Lake Lången in Skee parish, Bohuslän. The first finds from the site were collected in the 19th century. Alin summarized all known finds in 1955.

The settlements are coastal bound; however, a new element is that inland settlements are becoming more common. During the Late Mesolithic even the coastal areas are characterized by a broad leaved forest with oak, elm and lime. The Lihult sites have a very similar inventory at both the coastal and inland settlements. The flint inventory is characterized by micro-blades, handle cores, segment knives and Lihult axes (Fig. 54). This type of axe is made of stone with a polished edge. These are all present after *c.* 5800 BC. Handle cores are very common and keeled scrapers are present at about 90% of the settlements. In southern Scandinavia these are typical of the late Maglemose and especially for the Kongemose Culture.

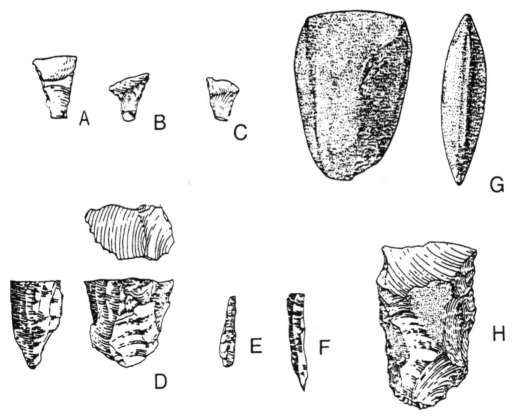

Fig. 54. Implements from the late Mesolithic transverse arrowheads group: a–c: transverse arrowheads; d: core; e–f: micro-blades; g: Lihult axe; h: flake axe (Source: Nordqvist 1997).

The Lihult sites are mostly situated in the outer archipelago and on small islands, except for sites in the northern part of Bohuslän where the they occur on larger islands at about 30–50 m.a.s.l. During this period the archipelago was even more pronounced with many islands, straits and bays. This was due to shore displacement with a higher sea level. It is obvious that the locations of the settlements were optimal for the procurement strategy of Mesolithic communities; fishing as well as hunting and collecting could be performed. From these sites we have only small amounts of bone which is a problem.

The first excavation of a Lihult site with preserved organic material was performed at *Rottjärnslid* in 1934 and 1944. The kitchen midden excavated here is till the largest on the Swedish west coast. It measured *c.* 4 × 6 m with a 250 m² large settlement surrounding it. The flint inventory has all of the artefacts characteristic for this phase. The bone material comprises both terrestrial and marine animals like roe deer, red deer and elk as well as fish like cod, ling and haddock. Shells from oysters and mussels were, of course, also present in the midden. It is obvious that marine species dominate in the assemblage.

A very interesting question is why are there so many Lihult axes deposited on some sites? We suggest two possible answers to this.

1. They are aggregation sites for a larger group of people.
2. They represent a type of burial site.

There are, as mentioned above, very few Mesolithic burials in the region. In interpretation could be that the dead were placed on a wooden platform or on the ground. The only element that would survive today would be the axe. As we will see in a later Chapter about Eastern Middle Sweden, we might have the same phenomena there in the Late Mesolithic.

A site with a lot of organic material is *Huseby klev*. This site was discussed above but the focus here is on a separate site that was situated a little bit further up in the valley. The site comprised a kitchen midden with oysters. This was only *c.* 1 m² and was covered by a 1 m thick layer of gravel mixed with shells. The midden was situated at the end of a rounded 6.0 × 4.5 m, large sunken structure. This was actually made up of a couple of smaller areas with shells and appears to have been a dwelling. Close by, an area with soot and ash was found. This was probably a hearth.

Most of the finds were discovered inside the hut and comprised much flint and, most important, organic material. The flint material is characteristic of an earlier part of the Lihult Culture. Some bone and antler fish hooks were found. Evidence for hunting and fishing is mostly made up of bones from fish, above all cod and haddock. Of terrestrial animals we have a lot of roe deer but red deer and wild boar are also present. The site with the dwelling belongs to the early phase of the Lihult Culture and is dated to the interval *c.* 6000–5700 BC – very narrow time margin that indicates a short-lived settlement.

Lihult inland sites

Do we then have any Lihult settlements inland and what do they look like? An area inland that has been thoroughly investigated is the area around Alingsås east of Gothenburg. Several Lihult sites have been found through field walking, especially around *Lake Mjörn*, as well as other smaller lakes. Very few have been excavated though. The settlement system during the Late Mesolithic could, according to Stina Andersson and Johan Wigforss in a publication from 2004, be characterized as follows: we have a large population in the coastal areas and in the archipelago. People could have lived here during the whole year, which the procurement strategy clearly shows; there would have been no need for any seasonal movement between the coast and inland. It is also interesting to note that there is a marked discrepancy between coastal and inland sites in the toolkit. At the coastal sites segment knives are very common while they are more or less missing on the inland sites. Another example, the core axe, is also missing inland while it is very common on the coastal sites. The inland and coastal groups would have led separate lives with different strategies and traditions.

As a rule, inland settlements are located near larger bodies of water. Waterways have been important in allowing people to move between different locations and settlements as well as for simple ecological reasons. Via waterways, people with boats have been able to access more ecological zones, something that is beneficial in many ways, for example in making and maintaining contacts and for hunting/fishing. However the strange thing is that they actually did not communicate. Maybe this was due to different tribal situations or social differences.

Transverse arrowheads

It appears that the Lihult settlements disappear around 4500 BC and a new group emerges – evidenced by the first transverse arrowhead settlements in Bohuslän and in northern Halland. Flake axes, handle cores and transverse arrowheads have been recovered from these sites.

Those that have been investigated so far seem to be quite small and located in exposed, westerly locations. The oldest of these is radiocarbon dated to *c.* 4600–4500 BC. There are, however, very few sites from the youngest phase, *c.* 4600–3800 BC.

It is interesting to note that the introduction of the transverse arrowhead cannot be compared directly with developments in Scania/Denmark, but comes significantly later. We can also note another difference – that the typical Ertebølle pottery is absent (Fig. 55).

However, regarding the Ertebølle Culture, it is interesting that we find typical Ertebølle objects in the form of, among other things, a Limhamn axe and transverse arrowheads at the *Breared* site at Varberg in Halland. Together with sherds from a characteristic Ertebølle pot (which was probably imported) from a nearby site also containing material with Lihult characteristics, these objects might indicate southern Scandinavian influences.

11   Moving North

It is now time to move north along the Mesolithic coast towards Uppland, Ångermanland and Dalarna. Seen from a regional perspective this area is, compared with the area south of Stockholm, not that well known. For many years the only Mesolithic site known here was Lilla Ramsjö outside Uppsala. The site was described, and partly excavated, by Gunnar Ekholm in 1910. After that a couple of excavations have been performed at the site. The difference in the number of sites is mainly due the substantial expansion in that area. During the last ten years or so this has started to change, however, not least due to the construction of a new motorway, the E4, through Uppland.

A moraine landscape stretches from Södertörn to the mouth of River Dalälven. The height above sea level is at most about 70 m. Several Late Mesolithic sites have been excavated along this moraine ridge. Sites like *Postboda 3, Lilla Ramsjö* and *Stormossen* are just a few examples. All of these sites are been located in similar coastal environment (Fig. 55).

The site *Lilla Ramsjö* might be a little different to the others. It has been interpreted as a large base camp situated between the coast and the inland and might have been a more complex site. With the help of radiocarbon it is dated to *c.* 5000 BC.

During the summer of 2003 five sites at *Stormossen* south of Tierp in northern Uppland were excavated. They have been called Stormossen 1–5:2. At the time of settlement this area was an archipelago with smaller and larger islands. The settlements are todya situated between 59–62 m.a.s.l. but in the Late Mesolithic the nearest main land was *c.* 20 km to the west. The sites varied in detail and assemblage composition and have been intrepreted as different types of site. They are all dated to just after 5000 BC (4700–4500 BC).

At the *Stormossen 5*, 1100 m² was excavated. The settlement was situated on a well-defined terrace facing south, in an area with large boulders. This terrace had a height abvee sea level of *c.* 63 m. No dwellings were found but the site was divided into two separate parts: one with hearths and one with cooking pits. If we look at the finds material it is totally dominated by quartz. Of flint we only have a couple of flakes and of rock flint (*Hälleflinta*) both flakes, cores and one micro-blade.

Economic indicators at the sites comprise bones from seal. About one-third of the bones are from seal. There are bones from larger herbivores as well and a large number of hazel nuts.

Nearby is the site of *Skallmyran*. The settlement is situated close to Uppsala Ridge, a long that stretches from south of Stockholm to the River Dalälven. The sites *Postboda* and *Stormossen* are also close to this formation. Skallmyran is located both on a plateau and on a northern moraine slope. Height above sea level is *c.* 55 m. No dwellings were found and thr only features were a couple of non-descript pits and a hearth. The finds assemblage from the site is quite

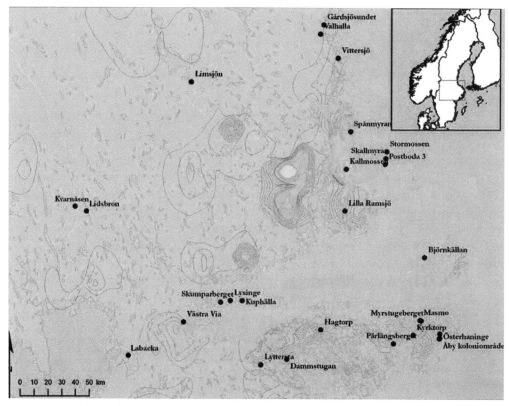

Fig. 55. Map of parts of Eastern Middle Sweden and the Baltic coast with the sites mentioned marked (Source: Guinard & Vogel 2006a).

small and more or less made up of quartz. There are no specific implements or other diagnostic pieces present in the quartz material. So, according to the excavators what we have here is a very short lived settlement, only visited once, and connected to a specific action. This is rather an unusual picture and thus interesting. The settlement should be dated to about the same time as Stormossen and a radiocarbon date indicates *c.* 4500–4100 BC. The date is uncertain as it is made on bone from seal and the marine reservoir effect is difficult to estimate here.

To summarize: the sites mentioned above all belong to the Late Mesolithic and seem to be rather short lived.

Leksand

At the time of deglaciation at the end of the last ice age (*c.* 9000–8500 BC), the sea, first Yoldia and later Ancylus, created a large lake with sweet water which, today, is Lake Siljan. Sea level at this time was *c.* 200 m higher than today. This is how the region appeared when the first pioneers colonized it. The oldest dated site is *Orsandsbaden* in Leksand (Fig. 56). A radiocarbon date on burnt bone produced a very early result *c.* 8500 BC.

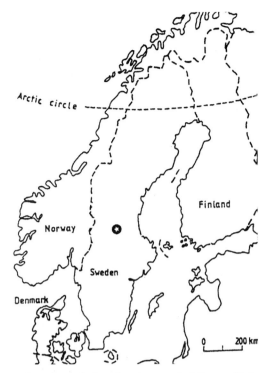

Fig. 56. Map of Sweden with the Leksand site marked (Source: M. Larsson 1994).

In 1984 a Late Mesolithic settlement site covering an area of about 1400 m² was excavated close to *Lake Limsjön* in Dalarna, central Sweden. The site is situated between 168.84 and 176.81 m.a.s.l. It is an important site for many reasons not least for the two, maybe three dwellings found at the site. The two best preserved are about 25 m² in extent. Their ground plans are oval in shape and they seem to have been sturdily built: a large number of stake-holes lined the wall (Fig. 57). It is interesting to note that there were hardly any finds inside the huts. Instead large hearths acted as focal points for the manufacture of tools and for subsistence activities such as the preparation of hides and food. The two, maybe three, huts seem to be organised in a semi-circle around an open area in the middle. Here we also have some hearths and many finds.

The total number of finds is very large, 15,799 implements, cores and waste were collected. The total weight is *c.* 23 kg. The number of implements is small though, only 108 have been determined and that is only 6% of the total number of finds. The material is clearly dominated by quartz. We have evidence, though, for the use of flint as well as local stone material, comprising porphyry, ash tuff, jasper and rock crystal. Of the implements it is important to mention the two handle cores found. They are of great importance for the chronology of the site (Fig. 58).

The climate of the period was warmer than today with a forest that included species like oak, elm and ash. This is clearly reflected in the osteological material from the site which

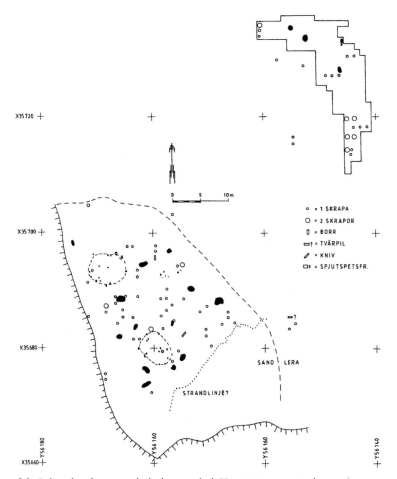

Fig. 57. Plan of the Leksand settlement with the huts marked. Key: 1, 2: scraper; 3: borers; 4: transverse arrowhead; 5: knife; 6: spearheads (Source: M. Larsson 1994).

consists exclusively of burnt material. The predominant species is wild boar but red deer, elk and smaller furred animals like otter and marten have been determined in the material. Fish are mainly represented by pike and the few birds which have been determined are dominaled by the duck family. The faunal evidence suggest that the site was occupied more or less all the year round, but chiefly in autumn and winter.

The dating of the site is not uncomplicated as there are several radiocarbon dates that indicate Iron Age activity. There is actually only one date that is Mesolithic, centred on *c.* 5690 BC. This is in good ageement with the common dating of the handle cores though.

In response to new development plans, a further excavation was made in 2012–13 which yielded a good result. The site was obviously larger than previously believed. No clear cut evidence for further dwelling structures was found but several radiocarbon dates clearly show

Fig. 58. Implements from the Leksand site: a–b: handle cores; c: flint scraper; d–e: keeled scrapers; f: fragment of slate dagger; g: scraper; h–i: quartz scrapers (Source: M. Larsson 1994).

three different settlement periods: 1. 7600–7000 BC; 2. 6600–6200 BC; 3. 5700–4400 BC. The last of these dates corresponds with the site with the dwellings.

Along the coast: further north

If we follow the River Dalälven from Leksand, and the sites mentioned above, we end up at the Baltic south of the city of Gävle. Few Mesolithic sites were known from this area but over the last ten years or so several new sites have been excavated. This is mainly due to construction work, new railroads and highways, If we can perceive Leksand as an inland site those I am going to discuss here should be understood as coastal sites.

Today the site of *Hästboberget* is located *c.* 107 m.a.s.l. The site was excavated ten years ago and it was the first to be excavated at this height. East of the settlement there was a mire that was possibly a lake at the time of settlement. Just a few features were discovered: hearths and small pits. The stone material was dominated by quartz. Interestingly, a handle core and a couple of micro-blades were found as well. If we look at the shore displacement curve, the site should be dated to *c.* 6800 and that is in good agrrement with the radiocarbon dates that place it at *c.* 6640–6450 BC.

In the summer of 1996 the Province Museum of Gävleborg (Länsmuseet Gävleborg) undertook an extensive archaeological excavation of a Mesolithic settlement at

Gårdsjösundet, in the parish of Skog in Hälsingland. This is the largest excavation of a Mesolithic settlement performed in this region. During the Mesolithic the site was situated on the southern slope of a narrow strait on a sandy slope facing north where it was protected by the high Nyängsberget mountain. The height above sea level was 106–116 m. The slope was divided into eight terraces or plateaus. These were separated by by seven natural embankments. As the sea receded, the settlement relocated further downhill, closer to the water. In total 53 features were registered. The largest group is made up of smaller or larger concentrations of brittle burned stone. No evidence for any dwellings was discovered during the excavation.

The finds material is very large, about 110 kg of worked stone was found. Half of it is made up of quartz and the other half of different types of volcanic rock. Flint is present but in very small quantities. The two whole blades discovered were probably imported to the site. It is interesting to note that three handle cores in different types of rock have been found at the site. A small number of so called keeled scrapers "*kölskrapor*" can be attributed to this group. The bone assemblage is small but for a site in this area actually quite large. It is clearly dominated by seal. There is evidence for elk, beaver and smaller furry animals as well. Fish and fowl are also present.

The dating of the site is, to a large degree, based on the seven radiocarbon dates performed on hazelnuts (5), burnt matter (1) and resin (1). The oldest dates are *c.* 7000 BC and these eminate from material recovered from above beach ridge V at *c.* 113 m.a.s.l. The youngest dates are I. 6400 BC and from an area situated *c.* 109 m.a.s.l. The dating of the site is, therefore, in good agreement with other sites producing handle cores.

Antother similar site is *Vittersjö*, excavated in 1994–95. The settlement area was situated on moraine on a slope towards the west. Today the remains are situated between 79 and 84 above sea level. During the Mesolithic the site have been on the western part of a large island. The settlement at Vittersjö comprises a very large area with remains of Mesolithic activities. During the excavation 79 features of different character were found. Most common were stake-holes, large and small, as well as roasting pits, hearths and waste pits.

If we look at the stone material it is obvious that quartz is most common followed by quartzite and different types of volcanic rock. Only one micro-blade in flint was found. No handle cores were discovered but keeled scrapers were present. Very few animal bones were found, possibly due to the morainic subsoil, but those that it was possible to identify were all from seal.

There is a marked difference in this site compared to Gårdsjösundet in that at Vittersjö four hut foundations were found. They are all made up of firecracked stone and sand. An embankment of sand and firecracked stone surrounded the foundations. Two of the huts was visible as cleared depressions on the slope. Within the embankments, diffuse stake-holes were discovered. The size of the hut foundations was *c.* 7 × 5 m and they were probably constructed as tents. In connection with these huts, roasting pits, heaths and waste pits were documented. Much of the finds material was discovered inside the hut foundations. According to the excavators, this might be an indication that the settlement was in use during winter.

The sites discussed above have been interpreted as settlement "areas" rather than formal settlements. People used these site seasonally and over hundreds of years. In response to shore displacement they repeatedly moved to be close to the shore. The sites are mostly seen as autumn/winter encampments for the hunting of seal. The hut foundations at Vittersjö could possibly lend some substansiation to this argument.

During the summer they moved inland to the lakes and rivers. In this context it is interesting to note that the distance to the site at Leksand is *c.* 90 km and it is quite possible that people could have migrated between the areas. The inland sites are located at 240–290 m.a.s.l. It is obvious that people preferred sandy beaches Unfortunately, we still know very litte about the sites and how they were organized. Looking at the stone material, it is clearly dominated by quartzite and quartz and little flint has been discovered here.

12   Pioneers in the Interior of Northern Sweden

During the last few decades, the view of the older Stone Age in Norrland has markedly changed. The interior of northern Sweden was the last area in Europe to become ice free and pioneer settlers arrived soon after deglaciation. To be able to cope with the variable environment the pioneers would have required a strong social and ideological framework, for both immigration initiatives and the enculturation of unfamiliar areas.

Three of the most important Stone Age researchers working in Norrland in the earlier part of the 20th century were Gustav Hallström, O.B. Santesson and Knut Timberg. Santesson discovered the first Stone Age site in Norrland in 1888, and hundreds of sites were to follow until he died in 1950.

In 1942 The National Heritage Board began its surveys and excavations in response to new lake and river regulations in connection with hydro-electric development in Norrland. These data have been treated in the project "Early Norrland" (*Norrlands tidiga bebyggelse*) and were published between 1972 and 1979. An important site for the discussion of the Mesolithic in Norrland was excavated at *Döudden*, Arjeplog parish, in 1958–59. This site is radiocarbon dated to around 5000 BC.

One of the most important, as well as the most discussed, excavations was undertaken in 1969 at *Garaselet* in Västerbotten, where the handle cores are particularly significant (see below).

In his survey of 1992, published in the book *Prehistory of Norrland* (1995), Evert Baudou wrote that knowledge about settlements in the interior of Norrland is poor, and the assumptions we make about how the society was organized is largely based on anthropological ideas about human social organization. Regarding hunters/gatherers, one often talks about band societies, which are loose societal organizations. During recent decades, knowledge about settlements and social organization has grown. This is chiefly due to the compilation of inventories, but also to the results of several archaeological excavations.

From seeing the region one which was more or less colonized fairly late, we now know better. Prior to 1999 there were only a very limited number of known sites (<5) dating to the Early Mesolithic. Now, as a result of intensive fieldwork in several areas, our picture of the Mesolithic in the interior of Northern Sweden is much altered.

The earliest sites

We have a couple of sites with very early dates from the northern most part of Sweden. One of perhaps four settlements in the area has been excavated At *Dumpokjauratj*, Arjeplog.

During the Stone Age Dumpokjauratj was a strait in a large lake that later became divided into several smaller ones like Hornavan. In the inner part of the bay several small islets existed.

The site was excavated over several years, the last season being in 2002. This was a rather limited excavation of 88 m². A couple of hearths and a waste pit were the only features. Compared to earlier excavations the finds assemblage was limited to some cores and micro-blades.

If we look at all the excavations undertaken here, the finds assemblage is quite largeoverall, comprising some 3500 artefacts. A slate knife and a tiny whetstone with two opposite scores for a hanging device are both artefacts unparalleled in Northern Sweden within such an early context. The raw materials used are of local origin, mainly quartz, quartzite, and fine-grained volcanic rocks. The extensive knapping debitage recovered shows that both platform and bipolar reduction strategies were used on all three groups of raw material.

No traces of any dwellings were found but it is obvious that there was some sort of inner deliberate layout at the site. This can be observed in the use of the features. It is, for example, obvious that each of the two settlement horizons identified, dated to *c.* 7600 BC and 7100 BC, are represented by a roasting pit. The excavated area exhibits three distinct clusters of finds material. In the areas between them, fire-cracked stones and burned bones are virtually absent and lithic material is sparsely scattered. It was around the roasting pits that most of the finds were made.

The spatial outline suggest that the Dumpokjauratj site served as a "residential base" inhabited during the summer season. Bones of young reindeer calves indicate that hunting and butchering occurred during the early summer, since calves are born in May. Furthermore, the roasting pits are indicative of outdoor activities during summer.

Other, contemporary sites in the surroundings show a quite different layout, with a single hearth or pit-hearth and no arefact material. These sites should perhaps be seen as sites used for short visits of special-task character.

Another site with very early dates was excavated in 2010 near the village of *Aareavaara* (*c.* 25 km north of Pajala). The northern part of Pajala is dominated by the valleys of the Torne and Muonio rivers. Between the rivers is a topographically flat to slightly undulating bedrock plain, in turn predominantly covered by flat till deposits (ground moraine) and, in depressions, extensive mires, all at altitudes between 160 and 220 m a.s.l.

It is interesting to note that the region where Aareavaara is situated marks the limit of where the ice stoped melting into the Ancylus Lake and, instead, melted onto terra firma. This happened at *c.* 170 m.a.s.l., which is the highest shoreline in the region. Dating when the icecap started to dissapear has proved to be rather difficult but sometime around 10,700 BP is a probable date. Associated with deglaciation of the area, melt water from the retreating ice formed a flat sand and gravel plateau east of Aareavaara village.

The size of the excavation at Aareavaara was very limited, less than 10 m². The stone material is dominated by quartz and a local type of slate. The people who lived here used the area seasonally and for short periods of time. They had the retreating ice cap in clear sight and stayed close to the shore of the Ancylus Lake. The little bone that was found indicates that they hunted small animals like beaver, but also reindeer. Reindeer is the most important prey on similar sites in Finland. As mentioned above, the dating of the site is not without its problems but, according to the excavators, a date around 8600 BC is very probable, based on radiocarbon dates. The dates from the site are more or less contemporary with the "Komsa Phase" sites on the north coast of Norway (~300–360 km northwards).

Antother recently excavated settlement with early dates is *Bölberget* in the province of Härjedalen. The site is located at a sandy plateau about 530 m.a.s.l. Below the plateau there is a vast area with myres and bogs. Strangely enough, there are no lakes or rivers in the viciinty of the settlement but this could be due to changes in the environment after that the ice cap melted away. The settlement is *c.* 75 × 30 m in extent and the excavation identified six concentrations of brittle, burned stone as well as an area with waste from the working of quartzite.

Three clear features were found. One, feature 2, is a roasting pit about 1 m in diameter. Feature 3 is a smaller, containing brittle burned stone and feature 9 is a large concentration of the same, 2 m in diameter. Feature 2 has been dated with radiocarbon (pine) to 7590–7510 cal BC, and feature 9 to 6810–6620 cal BC. This is also based on charcoal from pine.

It is interesting that there is about 700 years difference between the two features. They are, according to the excavator, quite similar so an interpretation could be that they are evidence for several visits to the site. The very small number of implements, or indeed waste, found at the site could suggest an interpretation of the site as a hunting camp. The stone material is local and made up of quartzite and porphyry which could also be seen as evidence for brief visits. It is worth mentioning that a keeled core, actually a handle core, was found during the excavation but it was, unfortunately, found in a secondary position without context. It is possible that it belongs to one of the settlement horizons.

In an interpretation of the site *Dumpkjaurati* immediately springs to mind. As we have seen, at that site two horizons, each represented by a roasting pit, were identified. At the site mentioned before there is a difference of *c.* 500 years between visits. Perhaps this is a common settlement pattern in the inner parts of Northern Sweden?

Later Mesolithic

In order to gain a better perspective regarding development in northernmost Sweden it is worth mentioning the sites with finds of so-called handle cores which, in southern Scandinavia, are usually placed in the middle part of the Mesolithic, and have been dated to *c.* 6000–4500 BC. The earliest date for a handle core in Northern Sweden is the find from *Högland*, southern Lappland, dated to *c.* 6600 BC It has often been argued that this rapid spread of handle cores can be connected to a migration of people from the Norwegian Trøndelag region. We can argue that the handle core tradition was spread from south to north through people moving in exchange networks. It is proposed that the handle core tradition carried values important for the reproduction of these societies. This is a very likely description of a complex course of events and, therefore, the blade core tradition can be associated with developments in southern Scandinavia.

In Norrland this form has been found at sites like *Garaselet*, excavated in 1969, in Västerbotten. The very early dates from the site, around 7000 BC, have been seen as the introduction date of the handle core tradition in Norrland. This is a multi-period site however, where the finds contexts are not as clear-cut as in Dumpokjauratj. There are remains from several time periods, from the Mesolithic up to the AD 1700s! However, Kjel Knutsson has emphasized that the blade core tradition in Norrland should perhaps be primarily connected with the later part of the Mesolithic, around 6000 BC. In southern Scandinavia handle cores are associated with the late Maglemose and Kongemose cultures around the same time as in Norrland.

To summarize this complicated issue, as there are two main schools of thought regarding the development of the handle cores.

1. One suggestion is that they represent migration/diffusion of ideas from south, south-west or west into Norrland.
2. The second school of thought emphasizes the easterly connections, and opens up the idea of diffusion from the east and north-east.

The conclusion of the above must be that the production of micro-blades on handle cores in northern Sweden belongs to the Middle and Late Mesolithic (Fig. 59).

During the period 5000–4000 BC, a transition took place from the use of dense fine-grained material such as *hälleflinta* (rock flint) and porphyry, to quartz. During the period 4750–4000 BC, we also begin finding bones from Eurasian elk and beaver at settlements. An interesting idea put forward by, among others, Kjel Knutsson is that the blade core tradition disappeared during this period and was gradually replaced by new shapes and materials,

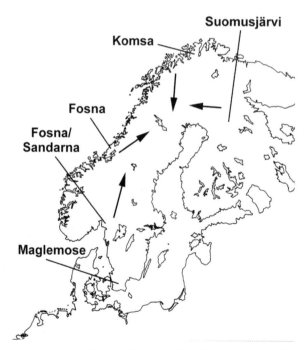

Fig. 59. Possible migration routes into Northern Sweden and neighbouring cultures (Source: Knutsson 1993).

shale for example, but also in the form of new kinds of semi-subterranean housing. Some argue that this had to do with people wanting to create a new and unique identity clearly differentiated from that existing in southern Scandinavia.

In the following section, some Late Mesolithic sites dated to the period *c.* 5000–4000 BC will be discussed (Fig. 60). Some of these even have dates that place them in the southern Scandinavian Early Neolithic. These dates are not, however, relevant in this context.

An intriguing new feature during the later part of the Mesolithic in Northern Sweden is the so called Semi-subterranean house ("*boplatsvall*" in Swedish) and sites with these structures are of special interest for our discussion, The semi-subterranean houses developed, to some extent, in the same way as did houses in the surrounding areas. To date, no studies have been done to confirm that this type of house was in use in the Norrbotten coastal area before 5000 BC. Around this time this type of dwelling is present near all river mouths and valleys in the area.

The first site of this type that we will look at is *Alträsket*. The semi-subterranean houses make up one special type of settlement. The oldest known examples have been excavated at this site (Fig. 61). They are both oval-shaped and measure 10 × 7 m and 12 × 7 m. Today they are located in a forested area at 98 m above sea level, but at the time of settlement they were on the coast. They have been dated to *c.* 5000 BC.

Vuollerim in Lappland is the second of these sites. The settlement, which included 3–6 hut foundations, is located at the confluence of the Greater and Lesser Lule Rivers. The excavated house, Norpan 2, appeared as a shallow oval depression, 12 m long (E–W), 5–6 m wide

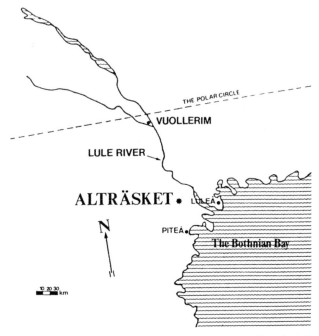

Fig. 60. Map of the northern Baltic coast with some of the sites mentioned marked (Source: Hallén 1994).

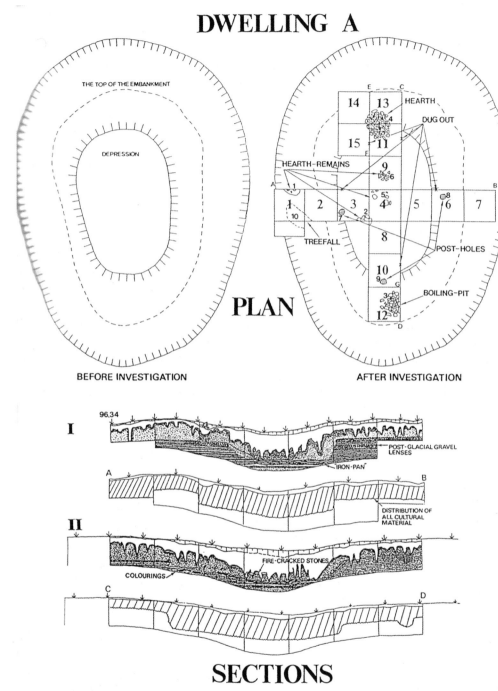

Fig. 61. A semi-subterranean dwelling from Alträsket (Source: Hallén 1994).

(N–S) and 25–35 long. The excavations revealed a rectangular floor, measuring 10.7–12 m by 4.2–4.7 m wide (Fig. 62). In and around this floor were variety of features, such as cooking pits and hearths. Especially notable is the 3 m long covered entrance along the eastern side of the house. A subterranean flue was discovered under this which led away from the fireplace, in other words, an early form of central heating. We can estimate the number of people living here to about 20–20. The site was probably only used during winter. In the surrounding area there is a large system with hunting pits and the burnt bone assemblage bears witness to the hunting of elk, beaver, sea birds and salmon. Dating analysis places the site at *c.* 4000 BC. Quartz dominateed the material tools were made from but stone and slate were also used. Taken together, this indicates a winter settlement. Evert Baudou claims that this is typical of base settlements in the inner coastal region.

The third settlement we will look at here is *Lillberget* at Överkalix in Norrbotten. The settlement belongs to the Comb Ware group, which has an eastern distribution. It was situated on a slightly sloping hill, *c.* 58–64 m above sea level, and had no direct connection with a larger body of water. However, near Lillberget there were a couple of smaller lakes and the settlement faces a larger wetland area. There are several interesting aspects to this site – nine dwelling structures and finds of comb pottery, flint, copper and a grave-field.

The nine, or possibly ten, dwellings are grouped around a *c.* 0.6 ha large depression that has a marsh-like quality. Interestingly, the houses are situated very close to each other. The houses vary in size between 21 × 13.5 m on the outside and 14 × 5 m on the inside. The smallest house is 8 × 7 metres and 5.5 × 3–5 m respectively. On the inside, the houses are almost rectangular in shape, with sharp corners. Their shape has led to the interpretation that they were probably built with logs as a kind of blockhouse. In addition, the floors are somewhat sunken. Several fireplaces were found in the houses.

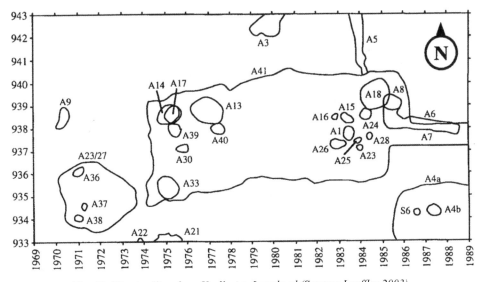

Fig. 62. The dwelling from Vuollerim, Lappland (Source: Loeffler 2003).

The eastern-influenced comb decorated pottery is the oldest in Northern Sweden and, like the entire Lillberget site, can be dated to about 3900 BC. As mentioned above, flint has been found here and is of a different kind than that found, for example, in Southern Sweden where the colour is generally greyish blue to black. That from Lillberget is almost light brown to greyish purple. What is interesting is that this type of flint originates from Russia. Also within the site is a small grave-field with four identified (probable) graves. I write "probable" as no human bones have been found. On what do we base this assumption then? The four shallow pits contain stones and traces of red ochre powder, which makes it possible to interpret them as graves. This is something considered typical for the Late Mesolithic graves at Skateholm in Scania and Vedbæk in Denmark.

Ove Halén, who excavated Lillberget, claims that the settlement should be seen as being permanently inhabited over a long time (1994). He also sees the choice of settlement location as strategic from several different points of view – communication, but also a rich abundance of game animals. What did the people hunt and eat at Lillberget? The clear majority (81%) of the burnt bones come from different species of seals, followed by European elk and beaver in significantly smaller amounts. Pike was the dominant species among the fish bone assemblage.

Epilogue

This has been an exhausting trip for all of us! Our travels have taken us from the southernmost parts of Sweden to the very north. Our trip began at a time when the ice cap started to melt in the south and ended up several thousand years later in Lappland. During the last decades several new and exciting sites have been discovered and excavated: Tågerup, Årup, Huseby Klev, Balltorp, Motala, the new sites in the East Swedish archipelago and, not least, the new discoveries of a couple of very old sites in Lappland. Taken together these sites have forever changed our perception of the Mesolithic in Sweden as well as in southern Scandinavia as a whole.

Many sites provide new information concerning dwellings, burials and subsistence strategies. I cannot help mentioning the hunt for dolphins on the Swedish West Coast. The newly discovered fermentation gutter in Blekinge also gives us a whole new image of the distant past. We can also observe how people came together, interacted, and performed rituals. The astonishing finds from Motala with the skulls on sticks are just one such place.

The establishment of networks both within Sweden and abroad is something that we have also observed. Contacts between different regions and people can be seen in, for example, the types and distribution of microliths, stone – and flint axes as well as bone/antler objects like slotted bone points.

I hope that I have managed to give at least an introduction to a very long, but also a very fascinating, part of our prehistory.

References

Aaris-Sørensen, K.E. & Brinch Petersen, E. 1986. The Prejlerup aurochs – an archaeozoological discovery from boreal Denmark, In Königsson, L-K. (ed.), Nordic Late Quaternary Biology and Ecology. *Striae* 24. Uppsala: Societas Upsaliensis pro Geologia Quaternaria, 111–17.

Ahlström, T. 2001. De dödas ben. In Karsten, P. & Knarrström, B. (eds), *Tågerup specialstudier*. Skånska spår. Lund: Arkeologi längs västkustbanan, Riksantikvarieämbetet, Avd. För arkeologiska undersökningar, UV-Syd.

Ahlström, T. 2003. Mesolithic human skeletal remains from Tågerup, Scania, Sweden. In Larsson, L, Kindgren, H. Knutsson, K., Loeffler, D. & Åkerlund, A. (eds), *Mesolithic on the Move; apers presented at the sixth International conference on Mesolithic in Europe, Stockholm 2000*, Oxford: Oxbow Books, 478–85.

Ahlström, T & Sjögren, K.-G. 2009. Kvinnnan från Österöd. Ett tidgmesolitiskt skelett från Bohuslän. Göteborg, *In Situ 2007/2008*, 1–18.

Ahlström, T & Sjögren, K.-G. 2013. Early Mesolithic skeletal remains from Bohuslän, Western Sweden. In Meller, H., Gramsch, B., Grünberg, J.M., Larsson, L. & Orschiedt, K. (eds), *Mesolithic Burials – Rites, Symbols and Social Organisation of Early Postglacial Communities*. Halle: Landesmuseum, 235–41.

Alexandersson, K. 2001. Möre i centrum. Mesolitikum i Sydöstra Kalmar län. In Magnusson, G. & Selling, S. (eds). *Möre: historien om ett småland: E22-projektet*. Kalmar: Läns Museum, 111–28.

Alexandersson, K. & Papmehl-Dufay, L. 2009. *Två stenåldersboplatser i Runsbäck*. Kalmar: Läns Museum. Arkeologisk Rapport 2009, 49.

Alin, J. 1935. En bohuslänsk kökkenmödding på Rottjärnlid, Dragsmark. *Göteborgs och Bohusläns Fornminnesförenings Tidskrift*, 1–42.

Alin, J. 1955. *Förteckning över stenåldersboplatser i norra Bohuslän*. Göteborg: Göteborgs och Bohus läns fornminnesförening, 5–30.

Alin, J., Niklasson, N. & Thomasson, H. 1934. *Stenåldersboplatsen på Sandarna vid Göteborg*. Göteborgs kungl. vetenskaps- och vitterhets-samhälles handlingar. Femte följden. Ser A band 3 No. 6. Göteborg: Elanders.

Althin, C.-A. 1947. Agerödsutgrävningarna: undersökningar av mesolitiska boplatser i Skåne 1946–47. *Fornvännen* 1947 (5/6), 248–353.

Althin, C.-A. 1954a. *The Chronology of the Stone Age Settlement of Scania, Sweden. 1: The Mesolithic Settlement*. Lund: CWK Gleerups.

Althin, C.-A. 1954b. *Man and Environment. A View of the Mesolithic Material in Southern Scandinavia Meddelanden. från Lunds Universitets Historiska Museum* 1954.

Ameziane, J. 2009. *Mesolitiska och neolitiska landskapsrum*. Jönköpings: Läns Museum Arkeologisk Rapport 2009, 38.

Andersen, S.H. 1975. Ringkloster: en jysk indlandsboplads med Ertebøllekultur, *KUML* 1973/74, 11–94.

Andersen, S.H. 1993a. Norsminde. A "Køkkenmødding" with Late Mesolithic and Early Neolithic Occupation. *Journal of Danish Archaeology* 8 (1989), 13–41.

Andersen, S.H. 1993b. Björnsholm. A stratified Kökkenmödding on the Central Limfjord, North Jutland. *Journal of Danish Archaeology* 10 (1991), 59–86.

Andersen, S.H. 2013. *Tybrind Vig. Submerged Mesolithic settlement in Denmark.* Moesgård: Moesgård Museum, National Museum of Denmark, Jutland Archaeological Society.

Andersen, S.H. & Johansen, E. 1992. An Early Neolithic grave at Bjørnsholm, North Jutland. *Journal of Danish Archaeology* 9 (1990), 38–58.

Andersson, H. 2005. Ristat i rader: två dekorerade hornföremål från mesolitikum funna i Motala, *Fornvännen* 2005, 5–12.

Andersson, S. & Ragnesten, U. (eds) 2005. *Fångstfolk och bönder. Om forntiden i Göteborg.* Göteborg: Göteborgs Stadsmuseum.

Andersson, S. & Wigforss, J. 2004. *Senmesolitikum i Göteborgs- och Alingsåsområdena.* Coast to Coast books 12. GOTARC serie C. Arkeologiska skrifter no. 58. Institutionen för arkeologi. Göteborg: Göteborgs Universitet.

Apel, J. (Ed) 1996. *Skumparberget 1 och 2.* Rapport Arkeologikonsult. Upplands Väsby.

Appelgren, K. 1995. *Lilla Åby. Arkeologisk undersökning.* Rapport UV Linköping 1995 (19). Linköping.

Arbman, H. 1947. 1946 års utgrävning i Ageröds mosse, Munkarps socken, Skåne *Fornvännen* 1947, 176–8.

Arne, T.J. 1905. Ett fynd från äldre stenåldern i Östergötland. *Meddelanden från Östergötlands Fornminnesförening.* Linköping, 10–27.

Arwidsson, G. 1949. Stenåldersfynden från Kams i Lummelunda. *Gotländskt Arkiv* 1948–49, 147–67.

Arwidsson, G. 1979. Stenåldersmannen från Stora Bjärs i Stenkyrka. *Arkeologi på Gotland.* Visby: Barry Press.

Bagge, A. & Kjellmark, K. 1939. *Stenåldersboplatserna vid Siretorp i Blekinge.* Stockholm: Wahlström & Widstrand.

Bailey, G. & Spikins, P. (eds). 2008. *Mesolithic Europe.* Cambridge: Cambridge University Press.

Baudou, E. 1995. *Norrlands forntid: ett historiskt perspektiv.* Umeå: CEWE förlaget.

Bergman, I. 1995. *Från Döudden till Varghalsen: en studie av kontinuitet och förändring inom ett fångstsamhälle i övre Norrlands inland, 5200 f.Kr. – 400 e.Kr.* Umeå: Archaeological Institute. Umeå University.

Bergman, I. 2008. Roasting pits as social space. The organisation of outdoor activities on an Early Mesolithic settlement site in northern Sweden. *Current Swedish Archaeology* 2007–2008, 7–14.

Bergman, I., Påsse, T., Olofsson, A., Zackrisson, G., Hörnberg, G., Hellberg, E. & Bohlind, E. 2003. Isostatic land uplift and Mesolithic landscapes: lake-tilting, a key to the discovery of Mesolithic sites in the interior of Northern Sweden. *Journal of Archaeological Science* 30, 1451–8.

Bergsvik, K.A. 2003. Mesolithic ethnicity. Too hard to handle? In Larsson, L., Kindgren, H., Knutsson, K., Loeffler, D. & Åkerlund, A. (eds). *Mesolithic on the Move: papers presented at the Sixth International conference on the Mesolithic in Europe, Stockholm* 2000. Oxford: Oxbow Books, 290–301.

Bille Henriksen, B. 1976. *Svœrdborg I. Excavations 1943–44. Settlement of the Maglemose Culture.* Arkæologiske Studier III. Copenhagen: Nationalmuseet.

Binford, L. 1978. *Nunamiut Ethnoarchaeology.* New York: Seminar.

Binford, L. 1980. Willow smoke and dogs' tails. Hunter-gatherer settlement systems and archaeological site formation. *American Antiquity* 45, 4–20.

Biwall, A., Hernek, R., Kihlstedt, B., Larsson, M. & Torstensdotter-Åhlin, I. 1997. Stenålderns hyddor och Hus i Syd- och Mellansverige. In Larsson, M. & Olsson, E (eds), *Regionalt och interregionalt. Stenåldersundersökningar i Syd och Mellansverige.* Stockholm: Riksantikvarieämbetet. Arkeologiska Undersökningar Skrifter 23, 265–97.

Björck, M., Björck, N. & Martinelle, K. 1999. *Vittersjö. En mesolitisk boplats.* Gävleborg: Rapport-Länsmuseet Gävleborg 1999 (9).

Björck, M., Björck, N. & Vogel, P. 2001. *Gårdsjösundet. En av de äldsta bosättningarna i Norrland.* Gävleborg: Rapport-Länsmuseet Gävleborg 2001 (3).

Björk, T., Knarrström, B. & Persson, C. 2015. *Damm 6 och Bro 597. Boplatslämningar och en hydda från tidigmesolitikum.* Blekinge: Blekinge Museum Rapport 2014 (14).

Blankholm, H.P. 1995. *On the Track of a Prehistoric Economy. Maglemosian Subsistence in Early Postglacial South Scandinavia.* Aarhus: Aarhus University Press.

Boaz, J. 1999. Pioneers in the Mesolithic. The Initial occupation of the interior of eastern Norway. In Boaz, J. (ed.), *The Mesolithic of Central Scandinavia.* Oslo: Universitetets Oldsaksamlings Skrifter. Ny Rekke 22. 34–52.

Boethius, A. 2016. Something rotten in Scandinavia: the world's earliest evidence of fermentation. *Journal of Archaeologcal Science* 66, 169–80.

Bokelmann, K. 1981. Duvensee, Wohnplatz 8. Neue Aspekten zur Sammelwirtschaft im Frühen Mesolithikum. *Offa* 38.

Bolin, H. & Edenmo, R. 2001. *Övre Grundsjön, Vojmsjön och Lilla Mark rapport över arkeologiska undersökninga.* Stockholm: Riksantikvarieämbetet.

Broadbent, N. 1979. *Coastal Resources and Settlement Stability: a Critical Study of a Mesolithic Site Complex in Northern Sweden.* Uppsala: Archaeological Institute. Umeå University.

Browall, H. 1980. *Mesolitisk stenålder vid Täkern, Östergötland.* Linköpings: Östergötlands och Linköpings Stads Museum.

Browall, H. 1999. Mesolitiska mellanhavanden i västra Östergötland. In Gustafsson, A. & Karlsson, H. (eds), *Glyfer och arkeologiska rum – en vänbok till Jarl Nordblad.* Göteborg: Gotarc Series A 3, 289–305.

Browall, H. 2003. *Det forntida Alvastra.* Stockholm: Statens Historiska Museum.

Browall, H., Persson, P. & Sjögren, K.-G. (eds) 1991. *Västsvenska stenåldersstudier.* Göteborg: Institute of Archaeology. University of Gothenburg.

Burenhult, G. 1982. *Arkeologi i Sverige. 1, Fångstfolk och herdar.* Höganäs: Wiken.

Burenhult, G. (ed.) 1997. *Remote Sensing: applied techniques for the study of cultural resources and the localization, identification and documentation of sub-surface prehistoric remains in Swedish archaeology.* Stockholm: Theses and Papers in North-European Archaeology 13.

Bröste, K. & Fischer-Møller, K. 1943. Koelbjerg skelettet. Et fund fra tidlig maglemosetid. *Aarbøger for Nordisk Oldkyndighet og Historie* 2, 211–31.

Callahan, E. 1987. *An Evaluation of the Lithic Technology in Middle Sweden during the Mesolithic and Neolithic.* Aun 8. Uppsala: Institute of Archaeology. University of Uppsala.

Carlsson, A. 2015. *Tolkande arkeologi och svensk forntidshistoria: från stenålder till vikingatid = Interpretative archaeology and Swedish prehistory: from the stone age to the Viking period.* Stockholm: Department of Archaeology. University of Stockholm.

Carlsson, T. (ed.) 2004. *Mötesplats Motala – de första 8000 åren.* Stockholm: Riksantikvarieämbetet.

Carlsson, T. 2007. *Mesolitiska möten: Strandvägen, en senmesolitisk boplats vid Motala ström.* Lund: Lunds universitet.

Carlsson, T. 2008. *Where the River Bends: under the boughs of trees: Strandvägen – a late Mesolithic settlement in eastern middle Sweden.* Stockholm: Riksantikvarieämbetet.

Carlsson, T. 2012a. *Mesolitikum och bronsålderi Stora Sjögestad, Linköpings kommun.* Stockholm: Riksantikvarieänbetet Rapport 2012 (68).

Carlsson, T. 2012b. *10 000 år vid Södra Freberga, Motala kn.* Stockholm: Riksantikvarieämbetet Rapport 2012 (142).

Carlsson, T. 2014. *This Must be the Place. Perspectives on the Mesolithic–Neolithic transition in Östergötland, Eastern Middle Sweden.* Stockholm: Riksantikvarieämbetet.

Carlsson, T., Kaliff, A. & Larsson, M. 1999. Man and the landscape in the Mesolithic: aspects of mental and physical settlement organization. In Boaz, J. (ed.), *The Mesolithic of Central Scandinavia.* Oslo: Universitetets Oldsaksamlings Skrifter, Ny Rekke 22, 103–31.

Cronberg, C. & Knarrström, B. 2007. *Stenåldersjägarna.* Stockholm: Riksantikvarieämbetet.

Clark, J.G.D. 1932. *The Mesolithic Age in Britain.* Cambridge: Cambridge University Press.

Clark, J.G.D. 1936. *The Mesolithic Settlement of Northern Europe.* Cambridge: Cambridge University Press.

Cullberg, C. 1972. *Förslag till västsvensk Mesolitisk kronologi.* Göteborg: Institute of Archaeology. University of Gothenburg.

Cullberg, C. 1974. Cullberg svarar på Welinders kritik. *Fornvännen* 1974 (69), 155–64.

Darmark, K., Guinard, M., Sundström, L. & Vogel, P. 2009. *Svartkärret 1–3. Tre mellanmesolitiska lägerplatser i Närke.* Rapport SAU 2009.

Early Norrland 1972–1979. Stockholm: Kungl. Vitterhets-, historie- o. antikvitetsakad.

Edring, A. 2008. Två mesolitiska kustboplatser vid Yngsjö i nordöstra skåne. *Fornvännen* 103, 1–12.

En resa genom Närke i tid och rum-artiklar om arkeologin längs med E18 väster om Örebro. 2012. Skrifter från Arkeologikonsult nr 2. Upplands Väsby.

Eriksen, B.-V. (ed.) 2006. *Stenalderstudier: tidligt mesolitiske jægere og samlere i Sydskandinavien.* Højbjerg: Jysk arkæologisk selskab.

Eriksen, B.-V. 2013. Grave matters in Southern Scandinavia. Mortuary practice and ritual behaviour of the Maglemose people. In Meller, H., Gramsch, B., Grünberg, J.M., Larsson, L. & Orschiedt, J. (eds), *Mesolithic Burials – Rites, Symbols and Social Organisation of Early Postglacial Communities.* Halle: Landesmuseum Halle, 56–71.

Eriksson, K., Persson, M. & Ulfhielm, B. 2008. *Arkeologisk forskningsöversikt över Gävleborgs län.* Gävleborg: Rapport Länsmuseet Gävleborg 2008 (5).

Eriksson, M. & Wikell, R. 2008. Skärgårdsliv på stenåldern. *Populär Arkeologi* 2, 23–34.

Fischer, A. (ed.) 1995. *Man and Sea in the Mesolithic: coastal settlement above and below present sea level: proceedings of the international symposium, Kalundborg, Denmark 1993.* Oxford: Oxbow Books.

Fischer, A., Olsen, J., Richards, M., Heinemeier, J., Sveinbjörnsdottir, A.E. & Bennike, P. 2007. Coast–inland mobility and diet in the Danish Mesolithic and Neolithic: evidence from stable isotope values of humans and dogs. *Journal of Archaeological Science* 34, 2125–50.

Florin, S. 1948. *Kustförskjutningen och bebyggelseutvecklingen i östra Mellansverige under senkvartär tid.* Stcokholm: Stockholm University.

Forsberg, L. 1985. *Site Variability and Settlement Pattern: an analysis of the hunter–gatherer settlement system in the Lule River Valley 1500 BC–BC/AD.* Umeå: Institute of Archaeology. University of Umeå.

Fredsjö, Å. 1939. *Tvenne västsvenska insjöboplatser från stenåldern.* Göteborg.

Fredsjö, Å. 1953. *Studier i Västsveriges äldre stenålder.* Lund.

Fromm, E. 1976. Beskrivning till jordartskartan Linköping NO. *Jordartsgeologiska kartblad skala 1:50 000. Serie Ae* 19. Stockholm: Sveriges Geologiska Undersökning.

Gendel, P.A. 1984. *Mesolithic Social Territories in North-western Europe*, British Archaeological Report S218 Oxford: Archaeopress.

Gejvall, N.-G. 1949. Skelettmaterial från Kamsgravfältet. *Gotländskt_Arkv_*XXI, 169–70.

Gejvall, N.-G. 1970. The fisherman from Barum – mother of several children! Palaeo-anatomic finds in the skeleton from Bäckaskog. *Fornvännen* 65, 281–9.

Gejvall, N.-G. 1979. Stenåldersmannen från Stora Bjärs i Stenkyrka. Arkeologi på Gotland, *Gotlandica* 14.

Gruber, G. (ed.) 2005. *Identities in Transition. Meolithic Strategies in the Swedish Province of Östergötland*. Stockholm: Riksantikvarieambetet.

Grøn, O. 1983. Social behaviour and settlement structure. *Journal of Danish Archaeology* 2, 12–32.

Grøn, O. 1995. *The Maglemose Culture. The Reconstruction of the Social Organization of a Mesolithic Culture in Northern Europe*. British Archaeological Report S616. Oxford; Archaeopress.

Grøn, O. 2003. Mesolithic dwelling places in south Scandinavia: their definition and social interpretation. *Antiquity* 77, 685–708.

Guinard, M. 2007. *Wibecks äng*. Uppsala: Rapport SAU 2007.

Guinard, M. &. Vogel, P. (eds) 2006a. *Stormossen. Ett senmesolitiskt boplatskomplex I den yttre uppländska skärgården*. Uppsala: SAU Skrifter 20.

Guinard, M. &. Vogel, P. (eds) 2006b. *Skallmyran. En senmesolitisk kustlokal i Uppland*. Uppsala: SAU Skrifter 14. Uppsala.

Gustafsson, P. 2006. Ett nytt land: tidigmesolitikum i Kolmården. *Fornvännen* 2006 (101), 233–44.

Göransson, H. 1988. *Neolithic Man and the Forest Environment around Alvastra Pile Dwelling*. Theses and Papers in North-European Archaeology 20. Stockholm: Department of Archaeology. University of Stockholm.

Haak, W. (*et al.*) 2015. Massive migration from the steppe was a source for Indo-European languages in Europe. *Nature* 14317, 1–14.

Hagberg, U.E. 1979. Den förhistoriska kalmarbygden. In Hammarström, I. (ed), *Kalmar stads historia* I. Kalmar, 17–89.

Hallén, O. 1994. *Sedentariness During the Stone Age of Northern Sweden: in the light of the Alträsket site, c. 5000 B.C., and the Comb Ware site Lillberget, c. 3900 B.C.: source critical problems of representativity in archaeology*. Lund: Department of Archaeology. University of Lund.

Hallgren, F. 2011. Mesolithic skull depositions at Kanaljorden, Motala, Sweden. *Current Swedish Archaeology* 18, 244–6.

Hallgren, F. & Fornander, E. 2013. Skulls on stakes and skulls in water. Mesolithic mortuary rituals at Kanaljorden, Motala, Sweden, 7000 BP. In Meller, H., Gramsch, B., Grünberg, J.M., Larsson, L. & Orschiedt, J. (eds), *Mesolithic Burials – Rites, Symbols and Social Organisation of Early Postglacial Communities*. Halle: Landesmuseum Halle, 156–92.

Hallgren, F., Bergström, Å. & Larsson, Å. 1995. *Pärlängsberget: en kustboplats från övergången mellan senmesolitikum och tidigneolitikum: Raä 143, Ene 4:92, Överjärna sn, Södermanland*. Upplands Väsby: Arkeologikonsult R. Blidmo AB.

Hanlon, C. 2003. *Årup. Boplats- och bebyggelselämningar från senpaleolitikum, tidigmesolitikum och yngre bronsålder*. Stockholm: Rapport Riksantikvarieämbetet 2003 (6).

Hanlon, C. 2004. The ever-changing Barum grave. *Fornvännen* 2004 (99), 225–30.

Hanlon, C. & Nilsson, B. 2006. Årup. Bosättning från tidigmesolitikum i nordöstra Skåne. In Eriksen, B.-V. (ed.), *Stenalderstudier: tidligt mesolitiske jægere og samlere i Sydskandinavien*. Højbjerg: Jysk arkæologisk selskab.

Hernek, R. 2003. A Mesolithic winter-site with a sunken dwelling from the Swedish West Coast. In Larsson, L., Kindgren, H., Knutsson, K., Loeffler, D. & Åkerlund, A. (eds), *Mesolithic on the Move:*

papers presented at the sixth international conference on the Mesolithic in Europe, Stockholm 2000. Oxford: Oxbow Books, 222–30.

Hernek, R. 2005. *Nytt ljus på Sandarnakulturen. Om en boplats från äldre stenålder i Bohuslän.* GOTARC. Series B, Göteburg: Gothenburg Archaeological Theses.

Hernek, R. & Nordqvist, B. 1995. *Världens äldsta tuggummi. Ett urval spännande arkeologiska fynd och upptäckter som gjordes vid Huseby Klev, och andra platser, inför väg 178 över Orust.* Göteborg: Riksantikvarieämbetet.

Högberg, A. 2002. Production sites on the beach ridge of Järavallen. Aspects on tool preforms, action, technology, ritual and the continuity of place, *Current Swedish Archaeology* 10, 137–62.

Holm, L. 2006. *Stenålderskust i norr: bosättning, försörjning och kontakter i södra Norrland.* Umeå: Institutionen för arkeologi och samiska studier, Umeå University.

Holm, J. & Lindgren, C. 2008. *Tre mesolitiska boplatser vid Fornvätterns strand. Riksväg 49, delen Stubbestorp-Gustavstorp.* UV Bergslagen Rapport 2008 (17). Stockholm: Riksantikvarieämbetet.

Jennbert, K. 1984. *Den produktiva gåvan.* Lund: Acta Archaeologica Lundensia 4 (16).

Jensen, J. 2001. *Danmarks Oldtid. Stenalder 13.000–2.000 f.Kr.* Copenhagen: Gyldendal.

Jensen O. Lass, Sørensen, S.A, Møller Hansen, K. (eds) 2001. *Danmarks Jægerstenalder – Status og perspektiver.* Hørsholms: Hørsholms Egns Museum.

Johansson, G. 2014. *En 10 000 år gammal boplats med organiskt material i Mölndal. Ytterligare en överlagrad Sandarnaboplats vid Balltorp.* UV Rapport 2014 (91). Göteborg: Riksantikvarieämbetet.

Johansson, G., Lindman, G. & Munkenberg, A.-B. 2013. *Stenålder i norra Bohuslän. Med arkeologiska undersökningar för E6 som grund.* Göteborg: Riksantikvarieämbetet.

Johansson, L.G. 1993. Source criticism or dilettanti? Some thoughts on "Scandinavia's Oldest House" in Tingby near Kalmar, Småland. *Current Swedish Archaeology* 1, 21–32.

Jonsson, L. & Gerdin, A.-L. 1997. *Bredgårdsmannen.* Arkeologiska Resultat. Göteborg: Uv Väst rapport 1997 (11).

Jordan, P. 2003. *Material Culture and SACRED LAndscape. The Anthropology of the Siberian Khanty.* Walnut Creek: Left Coast Press.

Jönsson, A. 2007. *Bölberget, en mesolitisik boplats i Härjedalen.* Östersund: Rapport Jämtli, Jämtlands Läns Museum 2008 (2).

Kaliff, A., Carlsson, T., Molin, F. & Sundberg, K. 1997. *Mörby. Östergötlands äldsta boplats.* Linköping: Riksantikvarieämbetet. Avdelningen för arkeologiska undersökningar. Rapport UV Linköping 1997 (38).

Karsten, P. 2001. *Dansarna från Bökeberg.* Stockholm: Riksantikvarieämbetet.

Karsten, P. & Knarrström, B. 1996. Norra Skåne – ett tidigmesolitiskt centrum. *Ale* 4, 1–10.

Karsten, P. & Knarrström, B. (eds) 2002. *Tågerup: specialstudier* 1. Lund: Riksantikvarieämbetet .

Karsten, P & Knarrström, B. (eds) 2003. *The Tågerup Excavations* 1. Lund: Riksantikvarieämbetet.

Karsten, P. & Nilsson, B. (eds) 2006. *In the Wake of a Woman: Stone Age pioneering of north-eastern Scania, Sweden, 10.000–5000 BC.: the Årup settlements.* Stockholm: Riksantikvarieämbetet.

Kindgren, H. 1991. Kambrisk flinta och etniska grupper i Västergötlands senmesolitikum. In Browall, H., Persson, P. & Sjögren, K.-G. (eds), *Västsvenska Stenåldersstudier.* Göteborg: GOTARC Serie C. Arkeologiska Skrifter 8, 38–71.

Kindgren, H. 1995. Hensback-Hogen-Hornborgasjön: Early Mesolithic coastal and inland settlements in western Sweden. In Fischer, A (ed.), *Man and Sea in the Mesolithic – Coastal Settlement Above and Below Present Sea Level.* Oxford: Oxbow Monograph 53, 201–13.

Kjellmark, K. 1903. *En stenåldersboplats i Järavallen vid Limhamn.* Stockholm: Antikvarisk tidskrift för Sverige. Utgiven af kongl. Vitterhets Historie och Antiqvitets Akademin 17 (3).

Kjällquist, M., Emilsson, A. & Boethius, A. 2014. *Norje Sunnansund. Boplatslämningar från tidigmesolitikum och järnålder.* Blekinge: Museum Rapport 2014 (10).

Knarrstöm, B. 2000a. Materialstudier av Skånes äldsta stenålder – om tiden efter Bromme och tidigmesolitisk expansion i norra Skåne. In Ersgård, L. (ed). *Människors platser – tretton arkeologiska studier från UV.* Stockholm: Riksantikvarieämbetet Arkeologiska Undersökningar Skrifter 31, 23–45.

Knarrström, B. 2000b. Tidigmesolitisk bosättning i Sydvästra Småland. In Lagerås, P. (ed.) *Arkeologi och paleoekologi i sydvästra Småland.* Lund: Riksantikvarieämbetet Arkeologiska Undersökningar Skrifter 34, 9–15.

Knutsson, K. 1993. Garaselet – Lappviken – Rastklippan: Introduktion till en diskussion om Norrlands Äldsta Bebyggelse. *Tor* 25, 34–51.

Knutsson, K. 1995. Mesolithic Research in Sweden 1986–1990. *Currrent Swedish Archaeology* 3, 7–27.

Knutsson, K., Falkenström, P. & Lindberg, K.-F. 2003. Appropriation of the past. Neolithisation in the Northern Scandinavian perspective. In Larsson, L., Kindgren, H., Knutsson, K., Loeffler, D. & Åkerlund, A. (eds), *Mesolithic on the Move. Papers presented at the Sixth International Conference on the Mesolithic in Europe, Stockholm 2000,* Oxford: Oxbow Books, 414–31.

Knutsson, K., Lindgren, C., Hallgren, F. & Björck, N. 1999. The Mesolithic in eastern Middle Sweden. In Boaz, J. (ed.), *The Mesolithic in Central Scandinavia.* Oslo: Universitetes Oldsakssamlings Skrifter 22, 87–123.

Kozlowski, S.K. 2003 The Mesolithic: What do we know and what do we believe? In Larsson, L., Kindgren, H., Knutsson, K., Loefller, D. & Åkerlund, A. (eds), *Mesolithic on the Move: papers presented at the Sixth International Conference on the Mesolithic in Europe, Stockholm 2000.* Oxford: Oxbow Books, xvii–xxxii.

Königsson, E.S. 1971. Stenåldersboplatsen i Alby på Öland. *Fornvännen* 1971, 34–46.

Lagerås, P. (ed.) 2000. *Arkeologi och paleoekologi i sydvästra Småland.* Lund: Riksantikvarieämbetet Arkeologiska Skrifter 34.

Lannebro, R. 1976. *Implements and Rock Material in the Prehistory of Upper Dalarna.* Early Morrland 4. Stockholm: KVHAA.

Larsson, L. 1973. Ulamossen. A Stone Age settlement with three separate occupation phases. *Meddelanden från Lunds Universitets Historiska Museum* 1971–1972, 5–16.

Larsson, L. 1975. A contribution the the knowledge of Mesolithic huts in southern Scandinavia. *Meddelanden från Lunds Universitets Historiska Museum* 1973–1974, 5–28.

Larsson, L. 1978a. *Ageröd 1: B–Ageröd 1: D. A Study of Early Atlantic Settlement in Scania.* Lund: Acta Archaeologica Lundensia 4 (12).

Larsson, L.1978b. Mesolithic bone and antler artefacts from Central Scania *Meddelanden från Lunds universitets historiska museum* 1977–1978 ns 2, 28–67.

Larsson, L. 1980. Some aspects of the Kongemose Culture of Southern Sweden. *Meddelanden från Lunds universitets historiska museum* 1979–1980 ns 3, 5–22.

Larsson, L. 1981. Human skeletal material from the Mesolithic site of Ageröd I: HC, Scania, Southern Sweden. *Fornvännen* 76, 161–68.

Larsson, L, 1982a. De äldsta gutarna. *Gotländskt arkiv 1982,* 7–14.

Larsson, L. 1982b. *Segebro: en tidigatlantisk boplats vid Sege Ås mynning.* Malmö: Malmö museer.

Larsson, L. 1983. *Ageröd V. An Atlantic bog site in Central Scania.* Lund: Acta Archaeologica Lundensia. Series in 8 (12).

Larsson, L. 1984. The Skateholm Project. A Late Mesolithic settlement and cemetery complex at a southern Swedish bay. *Meddelanden från Lunds Universitets Historiska Museum* 1983–1984, ns 5, 5–46.

Larsson, L. (ed.) 1988a. *The Skateholm Project I. Man and environment*. Stockholm: Almqvist & Wiksell.

Larsson, L. 1988b. *Ett fångstsamhälle för 7000 år sedan: boplatser och gravar i Skateholm*. Lund: Signum.

Larsson, L. 1989. Late Mesolithic settlements and cemeteries at Skateholm, Southern Sweden. In Bonsall, C. (ed.), *The Mesolithic in Europe: papers presented at the third International symposium, Edinburgh 1985*. Edinburgh: John Donald, 367–78.

Larsson, L., 1990. The Mesolithic of southern Scandinavia. *Journal of World Prehistory* 4 (3), 257–309.

Larsson, L. 1991. Symbolism and mortuary practice – dogs in fractions-symbols in action. Umeå: *Archaeology and Environment* 11, 33–8.

Larsson, L. 1994. The earliest settlement in Southern Sweden. Late Palaeolithic settlement remains at Finjasjön in the north of Scania. *Current Swedish Archaeology* 2, 159–77.

Larsson, L. 2004. The Mesolithic period in Southern Scandinavia: with special reference to burials and cemeteries. In A. Saville (ed.), *Mesolithic Scotland and its Neighbours*. Edinburgh. Society of Antiquaries of Scotland, 371–92.

Larsson, L. 2009. The Mesolithic in Europe – some retrospective perspectives. In McCartan, S., Schulting, R., Warren, G. & Woodman, P. (eds), *Mesolithic Horizons 1; Papers presented at the seventh international conference on Mesolithic in Europe, Belfast 2006*. Oxford: Oxbow Books, 11–31.

Larsson, L. & Seip Bartholin, T.-S. 1978. A long-bow found at the Mesolithic bog site Ageröd V in Central Scania. *Meddelanden från Lunds universitets historiska museum* 1977–1978 ns 2, 21–7.

Larsson, M. 1986. Bredasten – an Early Ertbølle site with dwelling structure in South Scania. *Meddelanden från Lunds universitets historiska museum* 1985–1986 ns 6, 5–25.

Larsson, M. 1994. Stenåldersjägare vid Siljan. En atlantisk boplats vid Leksand. *Fornvännen* 89, 237–50.

Larsson, M. 1996. *Mesolitiska och Senneolitiska boplatser vid Högby i Östergötland. Bosättningsmönster och materiell kultur*. Linköping: Riksantikvarieämbetet. Avdelningen för arkeologiska undersökningar. Rapport UV Linköping 1996 (35).

Larsson, M. 2003. Storlyckan. Investigations of an Early Mesolithic settlement site in Östergötland, Eastern Middle Sweden. In Larsson, L., Kindgren, H., Knutsson, K., Loeffler, D. & Åkerlund, A. (eds), *Mesolithic on the Move. Papers presented at the Sixth International Conference on the Mesolithic in Europe, Stockholm* 2000, Oxford: Oxbow Books, 414–30.

Larsson, M. 2007. Mesolithic episodes. Three Mesolithic sites in Eastern Middle Sweden. In Wadington, C. & Pedersen, K. (eds), *MesolithicSstudies in the North Sea Basin and Beyond*. Oxford: Oxbow Books, 40–9.

Larsson, M. 2014. *Paths Towards a New World. Neolithic Sweden*. Oxford: Oxbow Books.

Larsson, M. & Molin, F. 2001. A new world. cultural links and spatial disposition. The Early Mesolithic landscape in Östergötland on the basis of the storlyckan investigations. *Lund Archaeological Review* 2000, 7–23.

Larsson, M., Lindgren, C. & Nordqvist, B. 1997. Regionalitet under mesolitikum. Från senglacial tid till senatlantisk tid i Syd- och Mellansverige. In Larsson, M. & Olsson, E. (eds), *Regionalt och interregionalt. Stenåldersundersökningar i Syd- och Mellansverige*. Stockholm: Riksantikvarieämbetet Arkeologiska undersökningar Skrifter 23, 13–51.

Lidén, O. 1924. Boplatsen vid Gettersö jämte andra sydvästsmåländska stenåldersboplatser i belysning av de stora boplatsfynden i nordvästra Skåne. I. *Meddelanden från norra Smålands fornminnesförening VII*. Jönköping: Norra Smålands Fornminnesförening, 23–31.

Lidén, O. 1925. Värnamo för 4000 år sedan. I: *Värnamo hembygds- förenings årsskrift.* Värnamo: Värnamo Hembygdsförening, 10–13.

Lidén, O. 1932. En stenåldersby vid Flåren. I: *Värnamo hembygdsförenings årsskrift.* Värnamo.

Lindgren, C. 1994. Ett bipolärt problem – om kvartsteknologi under mesolitikum. *Aktuell Arkeologi* IV. Stockholm: Stockholm Archaeological Report 29.

Lindgren, C. 1996. Kvarts som källmaterial – exempel från den mesolitiska boplatsen Hagtorp. *TOR* 28, 29–52.

Lindgren, C. 2004. *Människor och kvarts: sociala och teknologiska strategier under mesolitikum i östra Mellansverige.* Dissertation, Stockholm University.

Lindqvist, C. & Possnert, G. 1997. The subsistence economy and diet at Jakobs/Ajvide and Stora förvar, Eksta parish and other prehistoric dwelling and burial sites on Gotland in long-term perspective. In Burenhult, G. (ed.), *Remote Sensing* Vol 1. Stockholm: Theses and Papers in North-European Archaeology 13a, 29–90.

Lindqvist, C. & Possnert, G. 1999. The first seal hunter families on Gotland; On the Mesolithic occupation in the Stora Förvar Cave. *Current Swedish Archaeology* 7, 15–38.

Location, selection and memory. Södetörn during the Stone Age 2010. Upplands Väsby: Skrifter från Arkeologi Konsult 1. Upplands Väsby.

Loeffler, D. 1999. Vuollerim. Six thousand and fifteen years ago. *Current Swedish Archaeology* 7, 89–106.

Loeffler, D. 2003. Some observations concerning the relationship between distribution patterns, floor size and social organisation. In Larsson, L., Kindgren, H., Knutsson, K., Loeffler, D. & Åkerlund, A. (eds), *Mesolithic on the Move: papers presented at the Sixth International Conference on the Mesolithic in Europe, Stockholm 2000.* Oxford: Oxbow Books, 239–49.

Lundberg, Å. 1997. *Vinterbyar: ett bandsamhälles territorier i Norrlands inland, 4500–2500 f. Kr.* Umeå: University.

Magnusson, G. & Selling, S. (eds) 2001. *Möre: historien om ett småland: E22-projektet.* Kalmar: Kalmar Läns museum.

Meschke, C. 1977. *Early Norrland sites on the Umeälven: a study of a cultural-historical survey.* Stockholm: Kungl. Vitterhets-, historie- och antikvitetsakad.

Milner, N. & Woodman, P. (eds). 2005. *Mesolithic Studies at the beginning of the 21st century.* Oxford: Oxbow Books.

Molin, F. 2003. *Tidigmesolitiska lämningar vid Trädgårdstorp, Linköpings kn.* Linköping: Rapport Riksantikvarieämbetet 2003 (26).

Molin, F. 2007a. *Mesolitisk hyddlämning vid Kv. Intellektet. Linköpings kn.* Linköping: Rapport Riksantikvarieämbetet 2007 (56).

Molin, F. 2007b. *Äldre stenålder i Jägarvallen, Linköpings kn.* Linköping: Riksantikvarieämbetet Rapport 2007 (10).

Molin, F. & Gumesson, S. 2013. How to settle the dead – burials on the Mesolithic settlement Motala, Sweden? In Meller, H., Gramsch, B., Grünberg, J.M., Larsson, L. & Orschiedt, J. (eds), *Mesolithic Burials – Rites, Symbols and Social Organisation of Early Postglacial Communities.* Halle: Landesmuseum Halle, 123–34.

Molin, F. & Larsson, M. 1999. *Mesolitikum vid Storlyckan – hyddlämning och fyndmaterial.* Linköping: Riksantikvarieämbetet. Avdelningen för arkeologiska undersökningar. Rapport UV Linköping 1999 (1).

Möller, P., Östlund, O., Barnekow, L., Sandgren, P, Palmbo, F. & Willerslev, E. 2013. Living at the margin of the retreating Fennoscandian Ice Sheet: The early Mesolithic sites at Aareavaara, northernmost Sweden. *Holocene* 23 (1), 1–14.

Nerman, B. 1912. *Östergötlands Stenålder.* Meddelanden från Östergötlands Fornminnesförening. Linköping: Östergötlands Fornminnesförening.

Nicklasson, N. 1965. Hensbacka. En Mesolitisk plats i Foss sn. Bohuslän. *Studier i Nordisk Arkeologi.* Göteborg: Arkeologiska Museet i Göteborg.

Nilsson, B. 1997. *Förhistorisk bebyggelse invid Mörrumsån – resultaten av arkeologiska utgrävningar vid Lönebostället.* Rapport över arkeologisk undersökning inom fastigheten Hästaryd 5 (17), Mörrums sn, Blekinge. Blekinge: Blekinge läns museum.

Nilsson, B. & Hanlon, C. 2006. Life and work during 5,000 years. In Karsten, P. & Nilsson, B. (eds), *In the Wake of a Woman: Stone Age pioneering of north-eastern Scania, Sweden, 10,000–5000 BC. The Årup settlements.* Stockholm: Riksantikvarieämbetet, 58–178.

Nilsson, P., Rajala, E. & Westergren, E. 2002. *Tingby 4:1 En kustboplats från mesolitikum.* Arkeologisk undersöknings rapport 2002 (7). Kalmar: Kalmar Läns Museum.

Nilsson Stutz, L. 2014. Mortuary practices. In Cummings, V., Jordan, P. & Zvelebil, M. (eds), *The Oxford Handbook of the Archaeology and Anthropology of Hunter-Gatherers.* Oxford: Oxford University Press, 1–14.

Norberg, E. 2008. *Boplatsvallen som bostad i Norrbottens kustland 5000 till 2000 år före vår tideräkning. En studie av kontinuitet och förändringar.* Umeå: Studia Archaeologica Universitatis Umensis.

Nordén, A. 1932. *Östergötlands äldsta stenåldersboplats.* Stockholm: KVHAA 37 (2).

Nordin, P. 2012. *Göteborg 330 – två mesolitiska hyddor och ett neolitiskt hus.* UV Rapport 2012 (148). Göteborg: Riksantikvarieämbetet.

Nordqvist, B. 1988. *Västsvenskt senmesolitikum i centrum.* Rapport UV 1988 (5). Göteborg: Riksantikvariembetet.

Nordqvist, B. 1997. Västkusten. In Larsson, M. & Olsson, E. (eds), *Regionalt och Interregionmalt. Stenåldersundersökningar i Syd- och Mellansverige.* Arkeologiska Undersökningar Skrifter 23. Stockholm: Riksantikvarieämbetet, 32–47.

Nordqvist, B. 1999, The chronology of the Western Swedish Mesolithic and Late Palaeolithic. In Boaz, J. (ed.), *The Mesolithic of Central Scandinavia.* Oslo: Universitetets Oldsaksamlings Skrifter Ny rekke 22, 235–53.

Nordqvist, B. 2000. *Coastal Adaptations in The Mesolithic. A Study of Coastal Sites with Organic Remains from the Boreal and Atlantic Periods in Western Sweden.* GOTARC. Series B. Göteborg: Gothenburg Archaeological Theses 13.

Nordqvist, B. 2005. *Huseby klev. En kustboplats med bevarat organiskt material från äldsta mesolitikum till järnålder.* Rapport UV Väst 2005 (2). Göteborg: Riksantikvarieämbetet.

Nordqvist, B. 2006. *Trollåsen – en 12 000 år gammal boplatslämning.* Rapport UV Väst 2006 (9). Göteborg: Riksantikvarieämbetet.

Olofsson, A. 1995. *Kölskrapor, mikrospånkärnor och mikrospån: En studie i nordsvensk mikrospånteknik.* Umeå: Arkeologiska studier vid Umeå universitet 3.

Olofsson, A. 2003. *Pioneer Settlement in the Mesolithic of Northern Sweden.* Umeå: Archaeology and Environment 16.

Pagoldh, M. 1995. *Arkeologisk delundersökning av en ca 9000 år gammal stenåldersboplats i Anderstorp, Småland.* Arkeologisk rapport 1995 (15). Jönköping: Jönköpings läns museum.

Papmehl-Dufay, L. 2008a. *Stenålder på strandvallen.* Kalmar: Kalmar Läns Museum Rapport.

Papmehl-Dufay, L. 2008b. *Ölands äldsta grav? Kulturlager och gravar från stenålder och järnålder.* Kalmar: Kalmar Läns Museum Arkeologisk Rapport 2008.

Papmehl-Dufay, L. 2013. *Åter till Tingbyboplatsen*. Kalmar: Kalmar Läns Museum Arkeologisk Rapport 2013 (2).

Persson, C. 2012. *Den hemliga sjön: en resa till det småländska inlandet för 9000 år sedan*. Göteborg: Göteborgs Universitet.

Petersen-Vang, P. 1984. Chronological and regional variation in the Late Mesolithic. *Journal of Danish Archaeology* 3, 21–45.

Pettersson, M. 1951. Mikrolithen als Pfeilspitzen. Ein Fund aus dem Lilla Loshults Moor, Ksp. Loshult, Skåne. *Meddelanden från Lunds Universitets Historiska Museum* 1951, 1–17.

Pettersson, M. 2006. Mesolitiska boplatser i Stockholms skärgård: fiske och säljakt på utskären under 10000 år. *Fornvännen* 2006 (101), 153–67.

Pettersson, M. & Wikell, R. 2012. *Topp 85. Ett tidigmesolitiskt fiskeläge med spår efter bostad, eldning och sälslakt*. Stockholm: Arkeologisk forskningsundersökning. RAÄ 610 Österhaninge socken. Arkeologihuset rapport 2012 (6).

Pettersson, M. & Wikell, R. 2013. Tidigmesolitiska säljägare i Tyresta för 10 000 år sedan. Späckbetong, gråsäl och tomtning på en kobbe i Ancylussjön 120 km från fastlandet *Fornvännen* 2013, 73–92.

Pettersson, M. & Wikell, R. 2014. Where sky and sea are one. Close encounters with early seafarers and seal-hunters off the Swedish Baltic coast. In Riede, F. & Tallaavaara, M. (eds), *Lateglacial and Postglacial Pioneers in Northern Europe*. British Archaeological Report S2599. Oxford; Archaeopress: 103–19.

Pettersson, O. 1997. *Tre senpaleolitiska flintslagningsplatser och ett område med härdar från yngre bronsålder-äldre järnålder*. Rapport UV-väst 1997 (5). Göteborg: Riksantikvarieämbetet.

Rajala, E. & Westegren, E. 1990. Tingby – A Mesolithic site with the remains of a house, to the west of Kalmar, in the province of Småland. *Meddelanden från Lunds universitets historiska museum* 1989–1990 ns 8, 5–31.

Risberg, J., Berntsson, A. & Tilman, P.K. 2006. *Strandförskjutning under mesolitikum på centrala Södertörn, Östra Mellansverige*. Upplands Väsby: Arkeologikonsult Rapport 2006 (2) 037.

Ritchie, K.C., Grøn, K.J. & Price, D.T. 2013. Flexibility and diversity in subsistence during the late Mesolithic: faunal evidence from Asnaes Havnemark. *Danish Journal of Archaeology* 2 (1), 34–41.

Rydbeck, O. 1945. Skelettgraven i Bäckaskog (sittande hukläge) och dess ålder. *Meddelanden från Lunds Universitets Historiska Museum* 1945, 1–44.

Rydbeck, O. 1950. Om nordisk stenålderskronologi och gravar med sittande hocker. *Fornvännen* 1950, 281–308.

Salomonsson, B. 1962. Some Early Mesolithic artefacts from Scania, Sweden. *Meddelanden från Lunds Universitets Historiska Museum* 1961, 5–27.

Salomonsson, B. 1965. Linnebjär. A Mesolithic site in South West Scania. *Meddelanden från Lunds Universitets Historiska Museum* 1964–1965, 5–32.

Salomonsson, B. 1971. Malmötraktens förhistoria. In: O. Bjurling (ed.). Malmö: *Malmö Stads Historia* I, 14–167.

Sarauw, G. & Alin, J. 1923. *Götaälvområdets fornminnen*. Göteborg: Göteborgs Stad.

Sjögren, K.-G. 1991. Om västsvensk mesolitisk kronologi. In Browall, H., Persson, P. & Sjögren, K.-G. (eds), *Västsvenska stenåldersstudier*. Göteborg, Institute of Archaeology: University of Gothenburg, 11–33.

Sjöström, A. 1997. Ringsjöholm. A Boreal–Early Atlantic settlement in Central Scania, Sweden. *Lund Archaeological Review* 1997, 5–21.

Sjöström, A. 2004. *Rönneholm 6–10, 12, 14 och 15: arkeologisk undersökning av ett mesolitiskt boplatskomplex i Rönneholmsmosse, Hassle 32:18, Stehag socken, Eslövs kommun, Skåne* (Rapporter från institutionen för arkeologi och antikens historia, Lunds universitet 1). Lund: Lunds Universitet.

Stenbäck, N. (ed.) 2007. *Stenåldern i Uppland: uppdragsarkeologi och eftertanke.* Uppsala: Riksantikvarieämbetet. UV GAL.

Strömberg, M. 1986. Signs of Mesolithic occupation in south-east Scania. *Meddelanden från Lunds universitets historiska museum* 1985–1986 ns 6, 52–84.

Taffinder, J. 1982. *The Stone Age in Southern Småland. A Presentation of the Existing Assemblages with Special Consideration of their Mesolithic Components.* C-uppsats i arkeologi. Uppsala: Uppsala universitet. Arkeologiska institutionen.

Wehlin, J. 2014. *Pionjärerna vid Limsjön.* Falun: Dalarnas Museum. Arkeologisk rapport 2014 (14).

Welinder, S. 1971. *Tidigpostglacialt mesolitikum i Skåne.* Lund: Acta Archaeologica Lundensia 8 (1).

Welinder, S. 1973. *The Chronology of the Mesolithic Stone Age on the West Swedish coast.* Göteborg: Studies in North European Archaeology 9.

Welinder, S. 1974. Kring västsvensk mesolitisk kronologi. *Fornvännen* 69, 147–54.

Welinder, S. 1977. *The Mesolithic Stone Age of Eastern Middle Sweden.* Antikvariskt arkiv 65. Stockholm: Kungliga Vitterhets Historie och Antikvitets Akademien KVHAA.

Wigforss, J., Lepiksaar, J., Olsson, I. U. & Påsse, T. 1983. *Bua-Västergård – en 8000 år gammal kustboplats.* Arkeologi i Väreverige 1. Göteborgs: Göteborgs Arkeologiska Museum.

Wikborg, J. (ed.) 2014. *Ett landskap i förändring. Påljungshage-forntid i Nyköpingstrakten.* Uppsala: SAU skrifter 22.

Wikell, R. & Pettersson, M. 2009. Entering new shores. Colonization processes in early archipelagos in eastern central Sweden. In McCartan, S., Schulting, R., Warren, G. & Woodman, P. (eds), *Mesolithic Horizons* 1. Oxford: Oxbow Books, 24–30.

Wikell, R., Molin, F. & Pettersson, M. 2009 The archipelago of Eastern Middle Sweden – Mesolithic settlement in comparison with ^{14}C and shoreline in: Crombé, P., Strydonck. M.-V., Sergant, J., Boudin, M, & Bays, M. (eds), *Chronology and Evolution within the Mesolithic of North-West Europe.* Newcastle: Cambridge Scolar Publications, 234–45.

Zvelebil, M. 1998. What's in a name: The Mesolithic, the Neolithic, and social change in the Mesolithic–Neolithic transition. In Edmunds, M. & Richards, C. (eds), *Understanding the Neolithic of Northwest Europe.* Glasgow: Cruithne press, 1–37.

Zvelebil, M. 2003. People behind the lithics. Social life and social conditions of Mesolithic communities in temperate Europe. In Bevan, L. & More, J. (eds), *Peopling the Mesolithic in a Northern Environment.* British Archaeological Report S1157. Oxford: Archaeopress, 1–27.

Östlund, O. 2011. *Aarevaara – Tidigmeosolitiska kustboplatser nära inlandsisen.* Norrbottens: Norrbottens Museum Rapport 2011 (24).

Österholm, I. 1989. *Bosättningsmönstret på Gotland under stenåldern: en analys av fysisk miljö, ekonomi och social struktur.* Stockholm: University of Stockholm.

Åkerlund, A. 1996. *Human Responses to Shore Displacement.* Stockholm: Riksantikvarieämbetet. Arkeologiska undersökningar Skrifter 16.